"It speaks to our helplessness when someone dies and provides honest answers to the questions that we are afraid to ask."
—Kathy Sandler, Program Director, Elisabeth Kübler-Ross Foundation

"*What Can I Do? Ideas to Help Those Who Have Experienced Loss* is filled with clear illustrations, helpful advice, and practical action steps that will bring solid benefit to all readers."
—Ted Nace, Guideposts Foundation, Pawling, New York

"This book offers a brave and honest window into a world that is seldom discussed—the painful yet absolutely normal world of grief that comes to each in their turn—and offers 'real-life' suggestions on how to help."
—Rev. Deborah L. Patterson, Executive Director, International Parish Nurse Resource Center

"Some authors write from theory, but not Barbara; she writes from experience! It's Barbara's firsthand encounters with loss that make this book come alive. She speaks from the heart to the heart of her readers. This book is a must read for anyone wanting to help, but wondering how?"
—Dr. Charles Moore, Former President, Northern Theological Seminary

"In *What Can I Do?* Barbara Glanz takes the hymn text, 'in deeds of love and kindness,' and offers practical ideas that readers can use to offer more compassion when grief impacts someone they know."
—Harold Ivan Smith, D.Min., FT, author of *When You Don't Know What to Say* and *Grievers Ask*

"*What Can I Do?* is born of the author's own grief and the helplessness her friends felt in trying to comfort her. This book is filled with practical-and unique-ideas for helping someone who is grieving a loss and will be a welcome addition to any caring person's library."
—Rev. Kenneth C. Haugk, Ph.D., is author of *Christian Caregiving—A Way of Life,* and executive director of Stephen Ministries (www.stephenministries.org)

"It is a fractional second when one confronts those who have endured loss and are grieving—a tiny split second in which most of us experience a sense of vacuum as to what to say—what to do—what actions to embrace. And, too often, we rely on inadequate clichés—even inadequate actions. Barbara Glanz has set out an impressive set of recipes as to what to do—what to say—how to be a genuine *comfort* source for those who are enduring loss. Not just tips—real, life-earned insights combined with Barbara's unique empathy, pragmatism, search for hope in all things. This book can be a . . . resource for any and all who wish to be substantive when reaching out to those who are enduring loss."

—Bob Danzig, Former CEO Hearst Newspapers, author, speaker, professor

"This resource is full of practical and insightful suggestions on helping and caring for others. It answers the question of 'What can I do?' in an insightful and loving way."

—H. Norman Wright, Grief and Trauma Therapist, Author of *Experiencing Grief* (B & H Publishing Group, 2004) and *Recovering from the Losses in Life* (Revell, 2006)

"'What Can I Do?' These four words are so simple and so direct that it's easy to underestimate how powerful they can be when asked of someone who is grieving the loss of a loved one. Very often when we encounter someone who is grieving, we are at a loss to express our sympathy in heartfelt, meaningful ways. But, in her new book, Barbara Glanz suggests that one of the best ways to support a grieving person is to joyfully remember and honor the one who has died. Her book is full of thoughtful and practical ways to reach out to those in grief and to help ease the pain of loss. After taking her suggestions to heart, you'll never again have to feel uncomfortable asking, 'What Can I Do?'"

—Paul J. Meyer, Founder of Success Motivation International, Inc., *New York Times* best-selling author

What Can I Do?

What Can I Do?

Ideas to Help Those Who Have Experienced Loss

Barbara A. Glanz

Foreword by Dr. Ken Druck

Augsburg Books

MINNEAPOLIS

What Can I Do?
Ideas to Help Those Who Have Experienced Loss

Unless otherwise marked, scripture quotations are taken from the *Holy Bible, New International Version*®, copyright © 1973, 1978, 1984 International Bible Society. Used by permission of Zondervan Publishing House. All rights reserved.

Scripture quotations marked NAB are from New American Bible, copyright © 1970 by the Confraternity of Christian Doctrine, Washington, DC, is used by permission of the copyright owner. All rights reserved.

Note: Every effort has been made to locate the authors and copyright owners of the material used in this book. If an error or omission has been made, please notify the author or publisher and necessary changes will be made in subsequent printings.

Large-quantity purchases or custom editions of this book are available at a discount from the publisher. For more information, contact the sales department at Augsburg Fortress, Publishers, 1-800-328-4648, or write to: Sales Director, Augsburg Fortress, Publishers, Box 1209, Minneapolis, MN 55440-1209.

Library of Congress Cataloging-in-Publication Data
Glanz, Barbara A.
  What can I do? : ideas to help those who have experienced loss / Barbara A. Glanz ; foreword by Ken Druck.
    p. cm. — (Lutheran voices)
  Includes bibliographical references.
  ISBN-10: 0-8066-5327-2 (pbk. : alk. paper)
  ISBN-13: 978-0-8066-5327-3
  1. Bereavement—Religious aspects—Christianity. 2. Church work with the bereaved.
  3. Lay ministry. I. Title.
  BV4905.3.G53 2007
  259'.6—dc22   2006034958

Cover design by Dave Meyer; Cover photo © Getty. Used by permission.
Book design by Michelle L. N. Cook

The paper used in this publication meets the minimum requirements of American National Standard for Information Sciences—Permanence of Paper for Printed Library Materials, ANSI Z329.48-1984.

Manufactured in the U.S.A.

10   09   08   07   06   1   2   3   4   5   6   7   8   9   10

Contents

Dedication

To my son, Gavin, and my husband, Charlie, without whose precious lives and deaths this book would not have come into being; to all the beautiful people who have contributed ideas to this book and to the memory of their dear loved ones; to my dear friend, Jeff Fendley, who has been praying for the publication of this book for two years; and most of all, to our heavenly Father, who has promised to reunite us all for eternity one glorious day.

Credits

My deepest thanks go to all the people who have shared their ideas to help lessen other's pain. Many of their personal stories have had to be shortened because of the length of this book; however, that does not lessen the legacy they are leaving as a result of the life and death of their precious loved one. I have shed many tears for these dear ones as I have been writing this book.

Since I began collecting material for this book in 2001 and many people's e-mails and addresses have changed since then, we were not able to locate some of the people who sent in submissions, so we have not used their names in the text. If one of these writings is yours and you would like us to use your name, please contact us at bglanz@barbaraglanz.com, and we will add it in subsequent printings.

I especially want to thank my assistant, Suzanne Myers, and Lynette Johnson from Augsburg Fortress for all the many hours they spent collecting the permissions for this book. Each submission was precious to me as I know it came from the depths of the person's struggles through the valley of grief and loss, so we have tried every avenue to find each person who wrote to me or whose words touched my heart on my grief journey. Please forgive us if we erred in any way.

Most of all, I want to memorialize each loved one represented in this book. Through their lives, however long or short, readers will learn of new and precious ways to help those around them find some peace in the midst of their pain, and that is the blessing of healing for us all.

Foreword

Our society is not "grief literate," although we live in a time of tremendous loss. The aging of our population, news of terrorism, along with death and destruction from natural disasters necessitate that we learn the ways of grief—and of hope. Too often our instinct is to hold back, where we are more comfortable, fearing we'll say or do the wrong thing. The clichés we learn, such as "she is in a better place" and "time heals all wounds," tend to upset rather than help those who are grieving.

Helping someone we love cope with a loss is an intuitive art. Most of us never are taught it, but it can be cultivated. Simply "showing up" for others, providing meaningful support, and practicing compassion in the face of loss are crucial. The infinite ways we can respond to a dear one's loss fill the pages of this warm and intelligent book.

So what can we do or say to bring understanding, compassion, and a glimpse of hope to others? Barbara Glanz tells exactly how to help someone we love survive a loss. The myriad of strategies, from gardening to selfless listening to cooking dinner, come directly from her life experiences. A bereaved mom and widow, Barbara understands what people want and need from family and friends in their darkest hours—and when they are ready to receive it. Her book is a rich guide to loving care—from the beginnings of grief with its excruciating pain, along a road map of depth and honesty to love and sweet remembrances.

We cannot gloss over or spiritually bypass grief any more than we can manufacture hope. These things come from courageously facing losses with strength and patience. Those who do emerge with a renewed sense of compassion, faith, love, and acceptance of life—on its terms, not ours. Being a loving, quiet, humble, accepting, healing presence may make the critical difference in a moment of suffering.

My dear friend, author Ken Blanchard, introduced me to Barbara Glanz. He knew that the two of us have been living parallel lives as bereaved parents, inspirational speakers, grief educators, and organizational consultants. Barbara's outstanding and important book is sure to touch the hearts and lives of many thousands of people for years to come. I am blessed and honored to call her "friend."

—Ken Druck, Ph.D., author, *Healing Your Life after the Loss of a Loved One* and *How to Talk to Your Kids about School Violence.* Founder, The Jenna Druck Foundation & Families Helping Families program (www.jennadruck.org)

Preface

Grief is not a sign of weakness,
Nor a loss of faith,
It is the price of love.
    —Author unknown

I am certainly well-qualified to write a book on loss. When I was fourteen years old, my grandfather had a heart attack and died on a family vacation. At that time he was the most important person in my life because he loved me unconditionally. At that difficult age it was devastating to lose the one person who truly believed in me with no reservations and especially to lose him so suddenly.

When I was twenty-seven, I lost my beloved mother-in-law to liver cancer. She was only sixty-four years old and was one of the most loving, giving persons I have ever known. I could not understand why she had to suffer for so long when she was such a good person. She adored our little son, Garrett, who was just turning two when she died. "Why couldn't she have lived long enough to watch him grow up?" I asked in my grief.

Little did I know that the next year would be the most devastating one of my entire life. In the spring of 1970 I became pregnant with our second child. I had an entirely normal pregnancy and never even took an aspirin. Our second son, Gavin Ward Glanz, was born on December 21. Everything seemed fine, and we called all the family with the news. Early the next morning our pediatrician came to tell us that he thought the baby had a congenital heart problem, and they were taking him by ambulance to Cook County Children's Hospital. Our hearts sank! Charlie went with the ambulance and called later that afternoon to tell me that our baby had died, they believed of hyaline membrane disease. He was buried on Christmas Eve. For over four years, I could find little joy in the Christmas season. After all, it celebrates the birth of a baby, and our baby had died.

The Easter after the loss of our baby, Charlie, Garrett, and I went to Harlan, Iowa, to visit my parents for the weekend. While we were away, the veterinarian suggested he keep our St. Bernard puppy, Nanna, to remove bags of fluid that had formed on her elbows from flopping down on our slate entryway floor. Soon after we arrived, my father told us that we were to call our friend, the vet. One-year-old Nanna had had a heart attack on the operating table that day during the procedure, and they weren't able to revive her. Now I had lost my other baby!

The following fall my father at age sixty-two died of a heart attack in the middle of the night, and six weeks later I found a lump in my breast. I wondered just how much grief one person could take.

The next twenty-six years were filled with many ups and downs. We lost my father-in-law, my grandmother, two precious friends, and suffered through several illnesses, hospitalizations, accidents, and teenage crises. And then, in 1999, devastating grief struck again! Charlie, my husband of thirty-three years, on a routine visit for a yearly checkup, was diagnosed with lung cancer. After surgery and radiation, we thought we had beaten it, but that fall the cancer came back with a vengeance. He started chemotherapy in September, they found brain tumors in November, he got pneumonia in January, and he died May 10, 2000. I had lost my best friend, partner, soulmate, and lover.

Who would ever have thought that at age fifty-six I would have lost a grandfather, a father, a son, and a husband?

In the fall of 1999 our middle daughter Gretchen had moved from Chicago to Portland, Oregon, and in August after Charlie's death, our son, Garrett, his wife, Ashley, and our little grandson, Gavin, who was named for our son who had died, moved from Chicago to Seattle, Washington, where Garrett was offered a wonderful job with Microsoft. Leaving them at the airport that day was one of the hardest things I had had to do since Charlie died—it was another good-bye. Then in October, my wonderful assistant of three years decided to take a full-time job. I felt as if I were losing everyone who was important in my life.

Finally, in December 2003, I sold our family home of twenty-seven years in Illinois and moved all alone to the beach in Sarasota, Florida. I had no idea what a hard move it would be! I knew only a handful of people there and, with my hectic travel schedule, it was terribly difficult to make new friends. I realized I had left *everything* familiar behind, so the first year and a half were again ones of deep loneliness and grieving.

Through all those many times of loss, however, I learned that even in the midst of the most devastating pain, one can find blessings. That is what this book is all about—*helping people find hope in the midst of their suffering.*

So many people in my life asked at these times, "What can we do?" I learned two things from my experience:

• I was hurting too much to even *know* what I needed
• I was so emotionally and physically drained that even if I did have a need, I did not have the courage to ask for help.

Since most people I knew, especially when I was in my twenties, had not experienced similar losses, they were extremely uncomfortable with my grief, and most of them simply stayed away. This caused me so much extra pain that it became a mission of mine to write this book. I began to think about the things people had done (or not done) for me.

After my husband's death, I realized how much I wanted to help the people in this world who simply do not know what to do when someone they care about has experienced a loss, whether it is the loss of a child, the loss of a spouse, the loss of a parent, the loss of a job, or the loss of one's health. The collection of ideas in this book is a legacy to my husband, my son, and to all the loved ones whose lives are celebrated in the stories of kindness and caring that people all over the world have shared with me.

My prayer is that you, the reader, will find specific ideas of things you can do to help those who have experienced a loss, and that as you give of yourself to the persons in pain, you will be blessed just as you have blessed them.

Barbara

—Barbara Glanz
6140 Midnight Pass Rd. #802   E-mail: bglanz@barbaraglanz.com
Sarasota, Florida 34242   Web site: www.barbaraglanz.com

A Note to My Readers

January 30, 2005

I have been wanting to write this book for over two-and-a-half years and most of the material has been collected for that long. However, for some reason I was just never able to make myself sit down and write—until January of 2005. On the weekend I finally started the book, I had an epiphany: the reason I could not write it before was because I had not worked through my *own* grief thoroughly enough to truly be able to focus on helping others. Perhaps this book will be a symbol of closure for me or at least a move to a new level of acceptance. It has been exactly six years this month since my husband was first diagnosed with cancer and four-and-a-half years since his death. At last, I am healed enough to be able to share with you so that you can help begin the long healing process for others.

I have been trying to make the best of grief and am just beginning to learn to allow it to make the best of me.
—Barbara Lazear Ascher

When you are in the dark, listen, and God will give you a very precious message for someone else when you get into the light.
—Oswald Chambers

Introduction

Grief is the price we pay for love. When we dare to love, we risk the pain of loss.
—Andrea Gambill

I'm tired. Too tired to dress. Too tired to bathe. Too tired to eat. Exhaustion is my middle name since you have left me here to live without you. My own reserve of energy's not equal to the tasks of normal living. I use it up just trying not to cry, just trying to convince myself that life is good, that God still holds the world in his strong hands. I'm filled with questions now for which I have no answers. I've not the energy to think! Life seems to be a sham—an endurance test and nothing more. I know my heart still pumps. My lungs still fill with air; my blood still circulates. My eyes and ears still funnel their impressions to my brain; yet, I am filled with pain, unshakable and heavily compressed within my soul.
—Shirley Ottman

What do we live for if it is not to make life less difficult for each other?
—George Eliot

How well this paragraph describes the state of someone who is grieving! As the friend or family member of a grieving person, it is important for you to know what to expect from them as you try to help. The best advice I can give to you is to have *no* expectations. Everyone grieves in a different way. However, there are some universal truths I have experienced in all my experience with those who have had a loss.

Grieving people have no energy to handle even the most simple tasks of daily living. As family and friends, it is critical for you to simply jump in and do what needs to be done. Don't ask; just tell them that you are going to help and then do it. It is vitally important for you to anticipate what their needs will be because they will not be able to think ahead or remember things. It meant so much to me when people just said they were going to do (something). I did not have to think, and I did not have to feel guilty—I just had to be accepting and grateful.

Grieving people experience "grieving brain." Just as chemotherapy causes "chemo brain," an inability to think clearly and to remember things, so does grieving. You may have to tell a grieving person something several times before it even registers. They hear the words but cannot process the thoughts. Do not get frustrated by this—just be patient and understanding.

Grieving people are completely focused on survival and cannot process most advice. The last thing a newly grieved person needs to hear is advice about how to handle their grief. After several months, perhaps they will be open to reading and listening to others, but at first they simply need to have someone near to listen, to cry with them, to hold their hand as they attempt getting through each day.

After our baby died, someone gave me a copy of a book by Jess Lair called *I Ain't Much, Baby, But I'm All I've Got.* In the book he talks about living five minutes at a time during a horrible period of grieving in his own life. Reading this was life saving for me! There were many days when I would think I could not get through a morning or sometimes even an hour, *but* I could always get through five minutes, and I consciously learned to live my life that way—just five minutes at a time. One of the special blessings to come out of this time was that because of this experience, I am always fully in the present. When I am with you, I am 100 percent with you, and that is true of every experience in my life. You can greatly help your grieving friend by sharing this thought with him or her.

Grieving people do not want to hear, at least in the first few months, about others' stories. So often people feel that if they tell a grieving person about someone else's problems that seem even worse than theirs, it will make them feel better. Please, *do not* do this! Whatever pain the person is feeling is completely overwhelming, and they do not need to hear about other's pain. Most of the time, it would not even register except to make them feel guilty and that is the last thing they need at this time.

Grieving people must be completely focused on self. Doing something for someone else is impossible for most people in the

early stages of grieving. In traditional America we have the idea that people should "pull themselves up by their bootstraps," and get over their suffering, move on with their lives, and usually, this happens by doing something for someone else. What everyone needs to realize is that the grieving person *cannot* do anything for anyone else. Survival for them must be completely focused on self.

A book that has impacted my life deeply is William Styron's book, *Darkness Visible*. It is the account of this Pulitzer Prize-winning author's battle with depression. For the first time, I realized the depth of helplessness depression causes, and it became clear to me, as well as from my own experience in grieving, that someone in the midst of grief simply cannot reach out to others. Sometimes in the first few days of the shock when there are lots of people around, there comes an inner strength that allows one to function at a more giving level, but that soon disappears when the reality of the loss sinks in. Suggesting to them to do something for someone else will only cause guilt and more pain.

Grieving people do not even know what they need, and even if they do, in most cases they don't have the courage to ask for help. The person in pain simply cannot think about the most ordinary of tasks and responsibilities, so asking, "What can I do?" is meaningless. They have no idea! And later as time goes on, they may think of some things that would help, and yet, just as I experienced, their guilt that they "should" be able to handle this by now or do this themselves keeps them from asking. Again, *just do it!*

If you are just too uncomfortable to reach out to the person, do something anonymously. Mary Nelson told me that after her husband died, she would sometimes find a bouquet of fresh flowers lying on the trunk of her car. It touched her deeply that someone was thinking of her.

Grieving people need *time*, and lots of it, to work through their grief. As I mentioned in my earlier note to the reader, it has been six years since my husband, Charlie, was first diagnosed with cancer, and finally, I have been able to write this book. When our little boy died and was buried on Christmas Eve, it took me at least four years to truly enjoy Christmas again. I will never forget the pain of an assistant minister at our church at the time coming over about six weeks after our son, Gavin, died and giving me a lecture about how it had been long enough and I should be "back to normal."

Be patient **with those who are grieving and allow them all the time they need to heal in their own way.** If you try to "hurry up" the healing, feelings will only get buried and this will prolong the process. The only way someone can move on with their lives is to let go of the past "as it was supposed to be" and reach out toward a new beginning, and this takes different lengths of time for everyone.

Because of our experiences, Mike Stewart, a speaker friend whose son died at age thirty of cancer, and I decided two years ago to write a program on change that helps people deal with their feelings as they go through any kind of a loss. Everything we could find on change dealt with systems and processes, and yet until people acknowledge and deal with their feelings, whether it is change in their personal lives or in the workplace, they will not be able to move forward.

Dealing with change or loss is like playing on the monkey bars. Until you let go of the last bar, you cannot move forward to the next one. So, the greatest part of our grieving involves "letting go," and that is one of the hardest things for us as human beings to do. There is deep fear in the unknown, so we seem to always want to hold onto "what was." This letting-go process takes a great deal of time, and lots of support is necessary as we move through what we call "the struggle." However, the end result is acceptance and the ability to move forward.

Grieving people need good listeners because they *need* to talk about their loved one who died. Often they will tell the same stories over and over again to help them remember the person, and all we need to do is listen. At other times we are afraid that if we mention the loved one, we will be causing the person more pain, and it might even make them cry. What we don't realize is that by *not* talking about the loved one, we are discounting the loved one's very existence and are causing the grieving person even more pain. It is extremely important to keep their memory alive by acknowledging the impact they had on many lives.

Our little boy died soon after birth, and during the time I was pregnant, I taught adult swimming lessons at the YMCA. My "condition" was *very* obvious! I will never forget the devastation I felt when many of the people in my classes as well as others in our village never even mentioned the loss of our child. They acted just as if nothing had happened when my world was crumbling down around me. For months I avoided going anywhere that I might see people who were not close, supportive friends. What I needed most were those who acknowledged our loss and allowed me to talk about our son.

There is a powerful poem titled, "The Elephant in the Room" which exemplifies the discomfort and pain most people feel when the loved one is not mentioned. The "elephant" is right there, but no one acknowledges it. They talk about the weather, work, everything else except the "elephant" in the room. Everyone knows it is there, everyone is thinking about it because it is a big elephant, but no one talks about it. In the meantime, the grieving person is thinking, "Please, please, say her name. Please let's talk about my child (the elephant in the room)." As the author says, ". . . if we talk about her death, perhaps we can talk about her life." Otherwise the person is being left alone . . . in a room . . . with an elephant! And that is precisely how I felt so many times when I met someone after both my husband's and my child's death. The "elephant" was right there between us, and yet, they were not willing or able to talk about it and as a result, I was left feeling even more alone.

We also must remember that tears are healing, and one of the greatest gifts we can give to anyone is to share their tears. I love the thought that "tears are the holy water from our deep place of loving." If we had not loved, we would not have tears, so learn to be comfortable with this precious expression of caring.

Share your own experience *only* if it truly is similar. One of the most hurtful things you can say to a grieving person is, "I understand how you feel." The *only* time this phrase might be acceptable is if you have had a similar experience yourself, and then you can be of great help and support to a person who has had a loss.

When our baby died, a woman in my church whom I had not known well before and who had also lost a baby, became my most important listener, counselor, and friend. She kept me from thinking I was going crazy because she had *been there* herself. Without her support, it would have taken me much longer to heal.

When my husband died, Cheryl Perlitz, a speaker friend, came to me immediately because she had lost her husband just four years before. We talked almost every day for weeks, and she was the only one who could truly understand all my guilt, fears, loss of identity, and need for support. Even though many other friends and family members cared deeply and did many wonderful things to help me through my grieving, Cheryl was perhaps the most instrumental in my healing because she not only affirmed all I was feeling, but she also gave me hope that I *could* get through this experience and go on with my life.

Grieving people need encouragement. One of the best gifts you can give a grieving friend is to support, encourage, affirm, and celebrate with them the "baby steps" they achieve in their process. Charlie and I loved to dance, and because we had a wonderful marriage and were best friends, neither of us ever wanted to dance with anyone else. After he died, I had a great fear that I would never be able to dance with another man. Knowing this, several of my male speaker friends made it their gift to me to be sure that I was asked to dance at one of our conventions the year after Charlie's death. This was a *huge* step for me, and they were there to help and cheer me on!

There are many kinds of losses people face in this life. Some are less traumatic than others, like graduating from high school and college, knowing that you will never experience your friends in the same way again; leaving home for the first time; moving to a new place; having children leave to start their own lives and families; changing jobs; retiring from a job you have loved; leaving a church or other organization that has been important in your life; breaking up with a boyfriend or girlfriend; witnessing the death of a friendship. A line from Charles Dickens' book *Great Expectations* has been deeply meaningful to me as I have faced those kinds of losses: "Life is made up of many partings welded together." So, even though we may have losses, they become a part of us and our experience forever and ever.

My friend, T. Scott Gross, shared his thoughts about another kind of loss and grieving: "Just in case you haven't thought of it, you can grieve even for someone who is living. . . . I realized a few months ago that I had gone through all the stages of grief over the loss of my relationship with my mom."

Other losses are permanent and change one's life forever: divorce, death of a parent or spouse or sibling, loss of a friend, loss of health, and even aging itself. One caution for all of us is not to judge the depth or seriousness of someone else's grief. After our child died, it literally hurt my heart when friends would complain about their children. I would think, "How can they complain? They are so very blessed to *have* their children!"

Then I read a beautiful passage in Victor Frankl's book, *Man's Search for Meaning,* the story about his time in the concentration camps during World War II. He describes suffering as being like a gas which is put into an empty chamber. That gas will expand to fill up whatever room there is in the chamber at that moment. The amazing "aha" for me was that although perhaps not of the same magnitude in terms of life changes, another person's suffering could be just as great as mine because, no matter what the issue was, it would expand to fill their entire being. This understanding has helped me to have much more compassion and not judge another's pain or compare it to mine, even when it seems like things could be so much worse.

Grieving is a world none of us wants to enter. However, only when we go *through* it can we find healing and new life. For those of us who are standing on the sidelines awaiting our turn, it *will* come, my friends. The very best we can do until then is to be there for our friends and loved ones who have found themselves on that terrible journey, to pray for them, to hold their hands, to listen to their hearts, to help them face the tasks of living, and to cheer them as they move slowly forward. Then our hope may be that others will be there to hold us up when our own journey begins.

There is a story of a woman who came to the Buddha seeking help after the death of her child and was told that, for healing, she need only find a mustard seed from a household that had never known sorrow. According to the story, she traveled over all the world in vain, never finding such a household. What did she find instead? She found understanding, compassion, friendship, and truth.

These gifts are what you, too, can find as you reach deep into your heart to help those around you who have had a loss.

The measure of loss you are experiencing is
Beyond my emotional comprehension.
Yet I ache with you and I
Long to lift your load.
Even while knowing that you alone must carry
One grief at a time to
The God of all comfort.
How I pray that He will lead you daily

To the storehouse of His
Grace, compassion, and healing.
And on that day when I need
Help through grief's dark night,
I pray that God will grant me
The tender gift of you.
    —Susan Lenzkes, *When Life Takes What Matters*

I have survived so much loss, as all of us have by now—my
parents, dear friends, my pets. Rubble is the ground on which
our deepest friendships are built. If you haven't already, you
will lose someone you can't live without, and your heart will be
badly broken; and the bad news is that you never completely
get over the loss of a beloved person.

    But this is also the good news. They live forever, in your
broken heart that doesn't seal back up. And you come through.
It's like having a leg that never heals perfectly—that still hurts
when the weather is cold—but you learn to dance with the
limp. You dance to the absurdities of life; you dance to the
minuet of old friendships.
    —Anne Lamott

1. Choose Your Words Carefully

My mouth would encourage you; comfort from my lips would bring you relief.
   —Job 16:5

When we honestly ask ourselves which persons in our lives mean the most to us, we often find that it is those who, instead of giving advice, solutions, or cures, have chosen rather to share our pain and touch our wounds with a gentle and tender hand. The friend who can be silent with us in a moment of despair or confusion, who can stay with us in an hour of grief and bereavement, who can tolerate not knowing, not curing, not healing and face with us the reality of our powerlessness, that is the friend who cares.
   —Henri Nouwen, *Out of Solitude*

A little girl lost a playmate in death and one day reported to her family that she had gone to comfort the sorrowing mother. "What did you say?" asked her father. "Nothing," she replied. "I just climbed up on her lap and cried with her."
   —Charles R. Swindoll, *Killing Giants, Pulling Thorns*

Remember that in helping someone get through the grieving process, silence can truly be golden. It is often more important to be concerned with what you *don't* say than with what you do say. Simply a hug or touching a hand is often the best gift we can give.

My friend, Rosemarie Rossetti, writes about her experience with words after a terrible accident in a column that she titled, "Words as a Catalyst to Healing":

As we all know, life can change in an instant. Many know this from personal experience. My life changed drastically on June 13, 1998, while riding my bicycle. Suddenly, a three-and-a-half-ton tree came crashing down on me, leaving me paralyzed from the waist down.

I was in a rehabilitation hospital for five weeks. Faced with a body that now had limited function, I deeply grieved my losses. Friends and family came to my aid to console, encourage, and share my pain. Their love helped me to reexamine my life and my purpose for living. Those who visited me in the hospital, and at home, greatly impacted my recovery. With the unique insights that I have about coping with change and dealing with adversity, I am often consulted. Many people ask, "What is the right thing to say when visiting someone who has just experienced a crisis?"

Words can get in the way of communicating. Our deepest emotions are hardest to express with words. Oftentimes nothing needs to be said. It is more important that we just be with the person we are consoling. To "be with" is to open your heart to their feelings. Being with a person may be as simple as standing by the bedside, looking into their eyes, and holding the injured person's hand.

You can interpret a person's emotions by looking at their eyes and facial expression. Feel with them. Allow your tears and their tears to flow. Embrace the person physically and emotionally. Be a comfort and offer a shoulder to cry on. Connect on a deeply personal level.

Be comfortable with the silence in the room. If something comes to you that you feel should be said at that time, let the words evolve. If the person who is injured speaks, listen and respond.

Allow the person to feel and to express anger, grief, frustration, and loss. Acknowledge that these are natural feelings in response to the situation. Be sympathetic and supportive.

If the person wants to talk about his or her injury and prognosis, actively listen. Ask questions to help understand. Encourage them to ask their medical team questions too so they can better understand their body and how it has been either temporarily or permanently affected. Discuss what lifestyle changes will be needed and what they foresee as future limitations. Help them to talk about how they will make the adjustments.

To help the person focus on more positive thoughts, steer the conversation to hopeful outcomes. Talk about the advancement of medical technology. Discuss others who have had tragedies in their lives and have made the necessary adaptations to overcome obstacles. Help them to see other times in their lives when an adversity has resulted in an opportunity and how the opportunity has led to personal growth. We can have a significant impact in restoring hope and boosting spirits. It is important that the person is able to visualize their future, plump with promise.

To assist in this strengthening of spirit, tell the person what personality qualities you have seen in them that will facilitate their comeback. Describe their essence. Let them know that they are the same person as before the crisis. Help them to understand that their positive attitude, determination, and tenacity shown in the past will help them to get through this tragedy. Help them to cope with the life changes they face.

Laughter has therapeutic value. Your humorous observations of the situation can lighten the tone of the conversation. Encourage the person to see things from a humorous perspective.

It is important for the person to realize that life has its ups and downs. Now is a down time that will likely turn around. The reality of today may likely change for the better tomorrow.

Talk about other times in their lives when they were able to endure, one day at a time. The person needs to go forward with this perspective and be open to possibilities. The person needs to avoid being resistant to the changes in life that must be made in order to move forward.

With love in your heart and a concern for the well being of another, you should feel confident entering the room of your friend or family member. The impact that you can have is more powerful than any medicine on the market. In return, the feeling you will experience after your visit, knowing you have helped in a significant way, will make your spirit soar.

© Rosemarie Rossetti. Reprinted with permission.

Pray for the Grieving Person
Perhaps the best gift we can give to someone is the gift of prayer. Many studies have been done recently to explore the power of prayer. In one instance researchers randomly chose two groups of

heart patients and assigned people to pray for the members of one of the groups. No one prayed for the other group (unless, perhaps, it was their own family and friends). Even though the prayed-for group did not know they were being lifted up in prayer, they recovered much more quickly than the control group.

In the National Speakers Association, an organization of four thousand speakers, coaches, authors, and consultants, we have an e-mail prayer chain, and anyone can request prayers at any time from anywhere in the world. When Charlie was sick and then subsequently died, I often sent daily requests to this group. I received many supporting and uplifting e-mail messages over those months, and we were blessed to have the ongoing prayers of many people whom I had never even met! I am not sure I could have made it through that difficult time without those precious prayers.

A person who faces the living losses of a husband with mental illness and a son who has gone to prison talks about the importance of prayer: "Care enough to pray with us, whether we be adults or children. Let us know in so doing that you care enough about us to usher us into the presence of a loving God."

Share Messages of Comfort
Jeff Tobe shares what comforted him:

> I found something *incredibly* helpful when I was grieving. . . . I realized that there is a huge difference in the words that people use to comfort you. *Many, many* people say they are sorry and they truly mean it—it just does not have any effect when you are so sad. But, those people who could relate something about the deceased—a memory, a story, a funny incident—made a *huge* difference. We need to know how the outside world saw our loved one. When my dad passed away, one of my cousins shared with me how "scared" she was of him growing up. When we talked about his external persona versus how he really was, we both had a great cry and it was wonderful.

Nearly a year after Charlie died, Margie Kruk, a client friend of mine who had just learned of his death, left me a voice-mail message that she was thinking of me. She said it made her feel so good to know that her little stillborn son was in heaven with

Charlie. Because she knew what a good, loving father he was, she knew that he would watch over her little one with special care. What a precious gift those words were to me!

She also shared something that was meaningful to her: "When we bury our parents, we bury the past. When we bury a spouse, we bury the present. When we bury a child, we bury the future."

Sheryl Nicholson of Palm Harbor, Florida, tells of what she said to a grieving friend:

> Aaron was my daughter's high school sweetheart and so his family was a big part of our life. When he lost his mom to ovarian cancer, I was traveling and not able to attend the funeral. Having two parents alive and well, I needed to know what to say besides, "I understand your loss," because I didn't. I also knew that he said the sentence that made him the saddest and most angry was when everyone at the funeral came up to say, "I'm sorry." He felt like it was a repeat tape recording and offered no comfort at all.
>
> After much consideration, I arrived at his house and with a hug said, "I can't imagine what this feels like. Know that I love you and whenever you want to talk, I have a listening ear and an open heart." He told me later, it was the best communication of comfort he had ever heard.

A friend shared these words which were of comfort to him, "Several years ago when my dad died, my cousin, who is a Dominican nun, said this to me: 'We've been praying *for* your dad; now we can pray *to* him.' What a blessing it was for us to think of him in this way."

When our little baby died, there were some words that were devastating and others that comforted me greatly. When people shared things like, "You never really knew him," and "You can always have another child," it made we want to scream because it was as if his life did not count at all. However, one person shared that she felt God had specially chosen us to be Gavin's parents because when a lifetime on this earth is so short, that little one needs a great deal of extra love, and she knew how deeply Charlie and I had loved this little one from the moment of his conception. Another person assured us of something that research has now proven to be true. He said he was sure that Gavin could hear our voices even in the womb, and he knew how much we loved him and how blessed we felt to be his parents. He then needed our support and prayers even more as he left this world to be with the Lord. Someone else shared this thought, "If Jesus came to you and asked to raise your child, as a person of faith, how could you tell him, 'No?'"

When Charlie was near the end of his life, my close friend, Steve Holtzer from Seattle, wrote us these lovely words which made us both smile:

> You and Charlie are both in my prayers daily, and even though I don't understand why things are turning out like they are, I know the Lord is still in control and will work things out for his glory. In a small way, it must be similar to what Jesus felt on the cross when he cried out to his father, "My God, my God, why have you forsaken me?" If Jesus did not understand, then we have to know there will be times when we don't either. One thing I do know, however, is that God our Father is not untouched by our pain. Just as the cry of his Son on the cross must have broken his heart, so, too, the cries of his children must break his heart. You know, just this second I had a delightful thought, which I would like you to pass on to Charlie. I know how he loves golf, and I am not a golfer. But I just thought that when we all get to heaven, I would like Charlie to teach me how to play golf. I actually think I could be pretty good, especially with such a good teacher! Well, that thought brings a smile to my face, and I think that is a good note on which to end!

Share Something That Has Been Meaningful to You

Roy and Irene Saunderson like to share a poem they found with friends who have had a loss:

> While we were traveling across the United States to go to western Canada, we stayed overnight in Grand Forks, North Dakota. We attended a church on Sunday and the women's group had a lesson regarding death and grieving. We saw this poem and the ascribed author in a nice frame. Both

Irene and I looked at this and thought it was a lovely idea. Now, two to three months after friends and family have lost a loved one, we make a copy of the poem and frame it. We tell them how much this poem has meant to us, and we hope it might bring a measure of comfort for them as well. Several months ago we did this for a neighbor of ours and they often refer back to this kindness.

Death Is Nothing at All
I have only slipped away into the next room.
I am I, and you are you,
Whatever we were to each other, that we are still.
Call me by the old familiar name.
Speak of me in the easy way
Which you always used.
Put no difference into your tone.
Wear no forced air of solemnity or sorrow.
Laugh as we always laughed
At the little jokes that we enjoyed together.
Play, smile, think of me, pray for me.
Let my name be ever
The household word that it always was.
Let it be spoken without an effort,
Without the ghost of a shadow upon it.
Life means all that it ever meant.
It is the same as it ever was.
There is absolute and unbroken continuity.
What is this death but a negligible accident?
Why should I be out of mind,
Because I am out of sight?
I am but waiting for you, for an interval,
Somewhere very near,
Just around the corner.
All is well.
　　　—Henry Scott Holland

Avoid Platitudes. Bring Tissues. Listen.

Debbie Preuss of British Columbia writes about what to say and not to say when someone has experienced a loss:

I have had much experience in my thirty-nine years with loss. I lost my birth mom at the age of sixteen months; she was only twenty-five. My little brother and I were adopted and raised by our grandparents. When I was thirteen, my "dad" was killed at work, and within a year, I would lose three more close relatives. I have lost many cousins, aunts, uncles, and friends in the subsequent years along with my "mom" eight years ago. During this time I have learned a lot about facing the loss of a loved one. One of the worst things to do is utter the platitudes, such as, "They're better off," or "You'll be together again," among others. They are trite and discount the person's pain.

Don't fill silence with meaningless words. Be aware of when silence is the best thing. Time spent in silence is important. Just knowing someone is there helps. Don't be afraid to cry. Bring tissues and bring an extra box to leave behind. Don't be afraid to bring up the loved one's name. When the person is talking, listen. It doesn't matter how many times you've heard the story, listen. This is part of the healing process. Don't say you know how the person feels. You never do; each situation is different.

Never Ever Discount a Person's Grief

Karen Mains, a Christian author and speaker, once talked about speaking words of life or words of death. When we discount someone's feelings, no matter how good our intentions may be, we are speaking words of death.

When their infant daughter was stillborn, Lanette Salisbury of Vancouver, British Columbia, shared how people's words hurt them and seemed to discount the existence of their child:

> It upsets me that people think that because our daughter was "just a baby" that somehow we don't miss her as much as we would have had she been older. We simply grieve different things than people who have lost someone who has been in their lives for a long time. For instance, someone who loses their older child will mourn and miss the child that they loved and got to play with and do all sorts of things with; but for us, we mourn for all the things that we didn't get to do with her.
>
> We mourn that we knew hardly anything about her or what she would have grown up to look like or be like . . . the list goes

on! I would just like people to know that our daughter *does* matter and she *is* a real person, and we would have loved to have had her in our lives for longer. Just because she is a baby doesn't mean that it is somehow easier to get over our loss and that somehow we were "less attached" to her.

Miscarriage is common, affecting at least one in five pregnancies, yet socially it is often taboo. Instead of support from friends and family, a grieving couple may find themselves up against a wall of silence. That little one was *their child* and that child has died, even before having the experience of joy in this life. That's difficult and it's hard sometimes to know exactly what to say under such circumstances. Here are a few ideas that might help:

- Start by telling them you were saddened by the news.
- Show genuine concern.
- Give them opportunity to express their grief.
- Don't say anything to devalue this pregnancy by saying they can have another child.
- Don't put a time limit on grief.

I love that many hospitals now have women who make tiny outfits to bury these little ones in so that their existence is recognized and valued. The Still Missed Foundation sponsors this activity and others to help the grieving parents. It is a wonderful place to be involved because so many of these young parents have no one else to minister to them.

A friend describes the grief she feels from the loss of her mother: "It is amazing the range of emotions that have played over me in this last year. Some threaten to steal my very breath away, others bring a smile, others bring tears, sometimes it is a settling of sadness, and always there is a fierceness in the missing of such a special person."

Meet the Person at Her or His Point of Need

Karen Rowinsky of Kansas City shares an unmet need she wishes someone could have recognized and helped with:

Max died after a six-year struggle. As he got more and more disabled, he and I discussed what I should do if he ever would lose brain functioning or quality of life. At the end he developed Legionnaire's disease and was in a coma. He might have survived, but the doctors couldn't assure me that he would have all his mental capabilities. He was on his second liver transplant, which was not working, and his kidneys were failing, and he was looking at dialysis and perhaps a kidney transplant. I realized that we were in the time that Max and I had talked about, and I decided to insist that his medical care providers let him go. He died three days later.

At the end he had been helicoptered up to Omaha from Kansas since his transplants took place there. After the decision was made to let him go, they didn't know how long it would take. I decided that I wanted to bring him back to Kansas so he could die there. The insurance company had just cleared flying him back in a helicopter with me when he died. I was on my way back to the hospital from the hotel. I arrived when his body was still warm, but he obviously wasn't there. The thing that I wish would have happened was in the weeks that followed, no one encouraged me to talk about the experience of making that awful decision nor did they ask me if I needed to talk about the experience of missing his death and what it was like to say goodbye to his body.

I know that those might have seemed like too intimate questions to ask so I decided that I would have to bring up the subject. But, each time I tried to talk about it, I could tell from their body language and response that my family and friends found it too uncomfortable. Even when I asked them to listen, they would try, but they seemed so weirded out by it, that I never went into the detail that I would have found therapeutic. If even one person would have had the courage and wisdom to insist I talk through what went on as many times as I wanted, I think the healing might have been a little easier or quicker. One of the many things I learned from this whole experience is that people do what they can do and most are so uncomfortable with their own mortality and that of their loved ones that they find it too hard to share intimately in another's loss.

Dr. Anju Tripathi Peters shares how men and women can have different needs and how important it is for us to be sensitive to their body language and other signals so we do not cause any more pain. Sometimes I have found it is best to simply ask if they would like to talk.

My husband and I could not agree on what we would have appreciated after our miscarriage. Here are two opposing views. I appreciated when someone else shared their miscarriage stories and listened to me. It helped me grieve and recover. My husband, on the other hand, wished people would not talk to him about it and offer their stories. We both agreed, however, that if we lost a loved one, it would be nice if family and friends stayed over with us especially if we were alone, since nighttime can be long if you can't fall asleep.

Al Lucia shared his thoughts on this idea from the perspective of a man:

A grieving person needs others but only in their own way. By that I mean the help has to be on the terms of the one experiencing grief. This may appear selfish, but at such times one finds it difficult to give. An example of how each person has different "terms" can be seen in the description of the weeks following my wife's untimely death.

I, for some reason, could not bear to see a picture of her or even hear her voice on a recording without an incredible emotional response. Her mother, however, immediately set up a kind of "shrine" to her in her home with many pictures, etc. This was a way for her to deal with her grief, but the very same activity caused me even deeper grief.

If you help someone at a time of need, remember to first try to learn the type of need they have and to not project your own value system into the equation—especially if you have not had personal experience with the grieving process. This may sound like you would be treading in a dangerous zone to provide help, but anything worthwhile is not easy and providing help at such a time is one of the most worthwhile things you will ever do. I will never forget or stop appreciating those who took the time to help me . . . my way.

The most important thing we can do to help grieving persons is to allow them to share what they are feeling, whatever that may be, in a loving, non-threatening, accepting way, realizing that this is just one place on their journey to healing.

She Understood
She closed her eyes,
Honoring my pain with her
Silence
And I knew she understood
    —Terri St. Cloud, *Bone Sighs*

2. The Blessing of Tears

There is a sacredness in tears. They are not the mark of weakness, but of power. They speak more eloquently than ten thousand tongues. They are the messengers of overwhelming grief, of deep contrition, and of unspeakable love.
—Washington Irving (1783-1859)

For in grieving we admit the truth—that we were hurt by someone we loved, that we lost something very dear, and it hurts us very much. Tears are healing. They help to open and cleanse the wound. . . . Grief is a form of validation; it says—the wound *mattered.*
—John Eldredge, *Wild at Heart*

So often when we are reaching out to someone who has had a loss, we feel that we have hurt them in some way if something we say or do makes them cry, and this becomes very uncomfortable for us. Please, dear reader, hear me when I tell you that you have given them a gift when you allow them to freely express their tears and an even greater gift if you are able to cry with them: "Tears are the holy water from our deep place of loving."

I have been thinking a lot about tears lately. These words about "tears being the holy water from our deep place of loving" struck me deeply when I first read them, and they have stayed with me ever since. I think too many of us in our world today are afraid to care, afraid to allow our hearts to open to that deep place of loving, afraid to commit ourselves to more than a superficial relationship with most people in our lives.

How many people do you love from that deep place?

Although we can experience the precious blessing of tears of joy when something touches us deeply, most of the time our tears come from a place of deepest pain. And our society today tells us to avoid pain at all costs. Therefore, we allow ourselves to become emotionally numb, robots going through the motions of life. We use our busyness as an excuse to bury our feelings. Even thousands of years ago, Socrates warned, "Beware the barrenness of a busy life." My belief is that until we truly allow ourselves to *feel*, we can never experience the fullness of life.

These last six years have been a time of great pain and sadness in my life, and at times all I prayed for was that the hurt and loneliness would just go away. And yet as I look back, I realize the gift those tears represented: *I had the courage to love from the deepest place of my being.*

Kahlil Gibran wrote years ago in *The Prophet* that the deeper sorrow carves into our being, we have that much more capacity to experience joy. Our tears, then, become an expression of who we are and how much we've risked opening our hearts to others.

How deeply do you allow yourself to love?

Holy water is water that has been blessed. As tears come because of our deepest caring, those tears, too, are blessed. *We are alive. We can feel. We care.*

Don't hold back your tears, but rather give yourself permission to take the risk of freely opening your heart. Yes, you will experience pain and heartache, loneliness and disillusionment and sorrow, but you will also experience a depth of love and caring and joy that will ultimately transcend the pain.

I truly believe that to love and have been loved at that deepest place is the greatest blessing we can either give or receive in this life on earth. Celebrate that love with those who are hurting by sharing their tears.

3. Think about Immediate Needs

In the first year or two following Jason's death, I felt myself in a zillion pieces. There was no me. I died when my son died. My ears were buzzing. I kept saying, "I don't know how to do this." But there's a lot of power in simply putting one foot in front of the other. You have to walk through the pain crying oceans of tears.
—Kathy Schuster

Journey one day at a time. Don't try to solve all the problems of your life at once. Each day's survival is a triumph.
—Rabbi Earl Grollman, *Living When a Loved One Has Died*

The best thing you can do to help a grieving person is to provide solutions to needs that occur right at the time of the loss. The grieving person or family cannot think of details. They are usually in a state of shock, so take over. Don't just offer; *do it!* The chances of you making a mistake in helping are slim, and the comfort you will bring by thinking ahead and jumping in will far outweigh any concerns the family might have about the choices you make. Do remember that although they need comfort and support, often just staying for five or ten minutes is more than enough.

Valla Dana Fotiades shares ways that people were there for her immediately after her husband's sudden death:

> At 5:30 A.M., about ten hours after John died, one of my dear buddies, my walking pal, showed up at my bedroom window, armed with two handfuls of coffee and bagels. I said, "I haven't slept all night." She responded, "I know. That's why I am here. Remember, I have been there." (Her husband died and left her widowed at age twenty-nine with a toddler to raise.)

The same morning, a few hours later, my mother-in-law, who was first widowed at the age of forty-seven, my same age, and her son, my brother-in-law, who had been fourteen when his dad died, showed up at the door with my two nieces who are my children's best friends. They stayed until about 5:00 that evening. When they were ready to go, my brother-in-law turned to me and said, "The girls, Kara and Justine, are yours for the week . . . they will help you, clean for you, make food, take messages, screen phone calls, comfort your children, do whatever you need." This was an incredible gift that I had no idea I needed until the people arrived in droves and calls were ringing off the wall. My younger niece, Justine, accompanied my daughter back to school, which made a difficult transition run more smoothly. Kara and Justine both had a reading at John's service. They were real-life angels!

Offer Phone Cards, Flowers from Home; Provide Baby-Sitting

Ana Tampanna shared what friends did for them: "Barbara, we have just had a devastating, multiple loss involving violence and murder! One of the most caring ways that a friend reached out to us was to send us phone cards for one thousand minutes. We had to make countless long distance phone calls, and this was a blessing. Another thing someone did was to send flowers to the room in which we stayed while attending the out-of-town funeral. They were lovely and reminded us of the support we had back home. Families with small children offered to provide play time for our five-year-old grandson throughout the week of the funeral."

Think about Laundry, Funeral Details, Pictures

Pam Blankenship shares all the ways friends helped them when a terrible accident occurred:

> We lost our darling son, Connor, on April 20, 2000, while on vacation in Florida. In a matter of seconds he got out of the house we were renting and fell in the swimming pool and drowned. He was just three weeks away from his third birthday. One of our friends who was on the vacation with us offered to do all of our laundry from our trip. While I would have never agreed to this

in the past, I said yes. She took all our laundry home, including our son's, did all of our wash and brought it back, laundered, ironed, and on fresh hangers. One of our dear friends went to the funeral home and helped us with the arrangements for our son's memorial. We were in such a state of shock and grief over his death that without her, I am not sure if we would have made it through. Another dear friend helped us look through photos of Connor and had two of them blown up to 11" by 17" size in one day for the memorial service scheduled for Saturday, the day before Easter. One of those photos now hangs in our home.

Arrange to Have the House Cleaned

Joanne Ax of Boise, Idaho, shared, "I know that when my brother-in-law passed away a few years ago, one of the nicest things done for my sister was four hours of house cleaning by a maid service. Someone called to ask her permission to send them. They just came in, dusted, vacuumed, cleaned the bathrooms, cleaned the kitchen counters and refrigerator, and generally made the house neat and clean for all the people who descended on her. It was a great help—they were professionals and were in and out—and she just didn't have to think about any household things."

Paper Products and Postage Stamps: Help While Respecting Privacy

Lynette Reick from Sioux Falls, South Dakota, shares special things their friends did for them:

> When my father died eight years ago, a dear friend of mine came to my mother's house when I was there and brought food, but also brought paper products—tissues, paper plates, paper towels, etc. She also knew there would be little grandchildren there so in the bag she had coloring books and crayons. These items that this dear friend, Judy Roth, had delivered were used with much appreciation. When my family had earlier received word that my father had had a heart attack and we needed to get to the hospital immediately, a friend of the family, Shari Braun, knew this had happened and that we were at the hospital. Later in the evening after we had found out that my dad had died, she knew we would be home shortly. She went to my mom's house, put on the

pot of coffee, made sandwiches, left some lights on in the house, and left. She knew we needed time alone as a family to deal with the shock. What a thoughtful and kind deed this was! Our postmaster in Warner, South Dakota, Roger Roth and his family, put postage stamps in the sympathy card they sent. What a great help that was when we sent out our thank-you notes.

Another person shared that a sister-in-law wrote and sent thank-you notes for her because it was just too difficult for her to do at the time. This is something anyone could offer to help with.

Offer Your Home and Help for Visiting Relatives and "Be There" When Needed

A person told me that the nicest thing someone did for her was to offer her house to the overflowing abundance of relatives visiting from out of town for the services. You may also offer your home for a meal for the visitors to help take some of the pressure off the grieving family.

Barry Pitegoff, who works as a volunteer with the Jewish cemeteries in Tallahassee, shared these ideas which have helped him:

Many bereaved have relatives flying in for a funeral. Get the names and phone numbers of some of them and take care of meeting them at the airport. It's okay if you don't know them; you can always hold up a sign with their names on it.

If you live in a city where the obituaries are published and the home of the bereaved does not have an intrusion alarm, offer to arrange for someone to have a car in the driveway of the home and to sit in the house during the funeral, just to keep the house occupied. There are still places where people read the obituaries to know when homes may be empty.

It is so important to just be there for the bereaved, especially at times when no one else considers. If they are going to the funeral home alone to make arrangements, offer to be there. Months later, when the bereaved needs to make arrangements for a monument or gravestone, offer to be there to help. Depending on the spiritual anchor of the bereaved and what it calls for, offer to help with the ceremony dedicating the monument/memorial.

Honor Their Faith Rituals

Barry Pitegoff also makes this suggestion about bereaved persons of different faiths: "If the one you are trying to comfort has a different spiritual anchor than you do, call a nearby house of worship of that faith and ask what is appropriate in helping the bereaved. For example, Jewish mourning rituals are often unfamiliar to non-Jews. Some of the rituals are the discouragement of flowers, the importance of letting the mourner speak first when making a condolence call, and all the kosher-type restrictions of what not to take to the home."

Listen Carefully for Unusual (and Sometimes Unspoken) Needs That Exist

Tina Kreminski from Westerville, Ohio, shared the following story of someone who really listened and then took action: "When my father passed away, I rushed home (long distance), not bringing any clothing appropriate for a funeral. An old friend who had heard about my father's death called to express her sympathy over the loss of my dad. I hadn't spoken with her or spent any time with her in years. During the conversation I must have mentioned the clothing concern, and she dropped everything in her schedule (husband, child, work) to take me out shopping that evening. It was so comforting to have a familiar face who knew the layouts of the department stores! I don't think I could have faced it alone. We haven't spoken since the funeral, but I will never forget her kindness."

During the last three months of Charlie's life we left our home in Western Springs, Illinois, to come to the little villa we had just bought in Florida, his lifelong dream place. While we were there, we went up to Moffit Cancer Center to see if they could help him any more. On the Monday Charlie went into the hospital there, our church in Western Springs sent a voice-mail message to all the congregation about the situation and mentioned that we were all alone down here. The pastor called and said that night a new couple in the church, who didn't even know us, called him and offered to pay for airfare for two people to come down to be with us. How about *that* for a blessing!

Organize a "Dinner Brigade"

Debbie Preuss suggests, "Organize a dinner brigade so the family doesn't have macaroni and cheese every night. Make something that will freeze in an appropriate size for the family. Have several meals delivered at one time, when company is overwhelming at first."

When Annie Gourley from Belfast, Ireland, suddenly lost her young husband, Johnny, her builder, Peter Beech, became her special angel. When she did not have the energy or the will to cook or even to see people, Peter would leave small plastic containers of home-cooked meals hanging on her doorknob or sitting on the doorstep. Annie lovingly called these "Meals on Wheels for Widows!" As a result, a lifelong friendship of caring has come from what was a tragic situation.

The other gift Peter has given Annie is to make her laugh. Not only is he a good listener, but he has helped her find humor in some of her darkest days through his use of expletives and other earthy Irish expressions. In Annie's typical Irish words, "He has put the craik back into my life!"

Meatloaf for Breakfast

Rita Emmett, a dear friend who writes and speaks on procrastination, tells the story of how a neighbor's meatloaf met their needs:

"Dad died today." My mother's call from Florida knocked the breath out of me and my knees buckled. Just six days earlier I'd returned from a stay with mom. We had visited dad every day in the hospital, and when I flew home, I reassured my husband and children that Grandpa was going to be fine. How could he die? I couldn't believe it, but there was no time to sit and wonder.

It was a frantic time . . . trying to get a flight out of Chicago's O'Hare on a cold, snowy day . . . settling down my kids and husband. Mom wanted a memorial Mass for Dad back in Chicago, and since there was no room in her small mobile home for all of us, she wanted me to come down alone. It broke my heart to say good-bye to my small children, but I reassured them that when Grandma and I came back, we would all attend Grandpa's Mass as a family.

I finally arrived at Mom's place late that night, and we sat until even later talking, crying, remembering, praying, planning his funeral, and all those things you do when someone you love leaves this earth. Your heart is broken. You're numb. Thank God for the numbness, because the pain is so piercing, so excruciating, you can't imagine what it would be like if you weren't in that blessed state of numbness and shock. It was almost sunrise when Mom and I finally went to bed. Then a few short hours later, we were awakened by someone knocking at the door. Mom's neighbor, Winnie, was on her way to work and stopped to give us something in a casserole dish. "My deepest sympathy," she said, "Here! Put this in the fridge. I made it for you last night." She hugged us and then she was gone. Mom and I peered inside and saw a huge meatloaf. "Well," I kidded, "It's 7:30 in the morning. How about some meatloaf for breakfast?" Mom said, "Blech—what a goofy thing to bring over at this hour. Meatloaf for breakfast sounds disgusting." So we laughed and shoved the meatloaf in the refrigerator.

Talking about her tough schedule during those weeks, as we drove home from the funeral parlor at the end of that day, Mom mentioned that she'd eaten almost all her meals at the hospital and hadn't been to the grocery store in ages. When we arrived at her home, we suddenly realized we hadn't had one thing to eat all day long and we were starving. We checked the fridge and except for some spoiled milk and a few bowls of green fuzzy unidentifiable "mystery meals," there was nothing there—nothing except that goofy ol' meatloaf. We pulled it out, and that evening we feasted on the most delicious meal in the world. Better than lobster, better than anything we could think of, that meatloaf—which early that morning had turned our stomachs—was nourishment and comfort and kindness all rolled together. Winnie, who herself had been widowed just a few months earlier, knew that at a time like this, besides the need for emotional and spiritual nurturing, we needed other nourishment too. And she knew that good old-fashioned meatloaf would bring us comfort and a smile; it was just the right thing to do.

To this day, when people I love experience a loss, not only do I pray and try to find words to comfort their souls, I remind myself that they could use some comfort for the body too—like that glorious comfort food meatloaf. And every once in a while, like Winnie, I too have to deliver it at the beginning of the day. I see the puzzled looks on their faces—and I just smile.

Recognize Their Need for Rest

Debbie Preuss says, "Realize there are times, especially in the early weeks of grieving, that the bereaved person needs rest. Offer to come over to answer phones and doors."

While there, you can help them with other overwhelming tasks like addressing and stamping thank-you notes.

Remember Butterflies!

Robin Maynard of Zimmerman, Minnesota, writes about the precious symbol of a butterfly that a family member chose:

> When my husband's mother died, our nephew, Timothy, did something that turned out to really help us with her passing. While making arrangements at the funeral home, Karen, Timothy's mom, was given the option of choosing a design that could be embroidered in the satin of the casket. Karen let Timothy decide. He chose a butterfly.
>
> While standing next to the casket to say our final words, I glanced at the monarch butterfly design. I thought of the phrase, "A butterfly goes wherever it pleases and pleases wherever it goes." Her life had symbolized that sentiment. Kevin, my husband, was a pallbearer so we were not able to ride to the cemetery together. It was difficult to not be able to be near him and comfort him. Upon leaving in the processional, I prayed deeply for Kevin and all of his family. I also asked all of the "why" questions. When I reached the cemetery, I concluded my conversation with God with, "I know you have a higher purpose for this loss and that you will help us through."
>
> As I stepped out of my vehicle, the entire section of the cemetery near my mother-in-law's plot was filled with monarch butterflies. I knew my prayer was heard. I found my nephew, hugged him and thanked him. As spring turned to summer, seeing beautiful butterflies grace the air has been a gentle reminder of life and love. Next spring, Kevin and I are going to plant a memorial garden with flowers that attract butterflies. Timothy's seemingly small decision provided a bright spot during our time of loss.

Offer Airline Tickets or Frequent Flier Miles

I was deeply touched when Scott and Melanie Gross from Center Point, Texas, offered as many airline frequent flyer miles as I needed to get any or all of my children home during the time Charlie was sick. As a result, they were all able to be with him when he died.

Be Aware of Financial Situations

Debbie Preuss reminds us, "Often when one spouse has died, the other is left with frozen bank accounts because they are in joint names. Offer help or a loan. Don't wait for them to call you. Reach out and call them."

Lanette Salisbury of Vancouver, British Columbia, shares the financial needs of a young family experiencing a loss: "Our daughter was stillborn in my thirty-eighth week of pregnancy due to unknown causes. We still grieve and mourn the loss of our daughter in our lives so I have made a memorial Web page in her memory. It would have been helpful for us if people had realized the financial burden a death puts on a family. I never knew until we experienced it ourselves all the expenses that come along with a funeral, plot, grave plaque, etc. We had so many flower arrangements that we had flowers in every room in the house (even the bathrooms!) and the flowers were appreciated, but we would have appreciated a donation toward our expenses so that we wouldn't have had that extra burden on our minds."

Share Vacation Days

In her newsletter for The Cancer Club, Christine Clifford Beckwith shares an idea to help friends diagnosed with cancer: "If you work with someone who has been diagnosed with cancer, offer to donate one of your vacation or sick days to the cancer patient to use as a day to recover from their treatments. Go in together with several coworkers until you have a full week of vacation days that can be offered to your friend. They will relish the time off work to catch up on sleep, recover from chemotherapy, or simply relax and enjoy a much-needed break. On the day off that you donate, send flowers to your friend and a cheerful note wishing them a wonderful day."

She suggests to the cancer patient: "If coworkers ask, 'What can I do to help?' suggest the donation of a vacation day to help you improve your mental health as well as the physical.

4. Anticipate the Person's Needs and Offer Practical Help

We need your hugs. We need your friendship. We need your love, kindness, and caring. We need your prayers. We need your understanding, not your rebukes and exhortations. Sometimes we need your advice and counsel . . . we will ask. We need help in practical ways. We just need you to hear us and accept us where we are. We need you. . . . Please be there to listen.

—A bereaved parent

Sometimes when we are grieving, we know what we need, and we also know that many of our friends would love to help us. However, we just do not have the courage to ask for that help. So you can be the one to anticipate the needs of the hurting person. Think ahead to what would help *you* if you were in that situation and do not wait for them to ask, because the chances are pretty good that they never will. When they are healed enough to have the strength to ask, they will have the strength to do whatever it is themselves.

Go to the Store for Them

I did not go to the grocery store for six weeks after Charlie died! I would stop at the gas station for milk and the convenience store for a head of lettuce or a few pieces of fruit, but I could *not* bring myself to go the grocery store. For one thing, that had become "his" job since he had retired to help me in my business, so it was painful to have to take it over. It was a reality I could not yet accept. For another, I knew exactly what would happen when I went. For the first four times I finally did go to the store, at least four people came up to me each time to ask how Charlie was doing. Of course, they were being kind, but it was like a knife through my heart each time I had to tell them that he had died.

If only someone had called and said, "Please get a grocery list together. I will be over tomorrow afternoon to go to the store for you," it would have been a huge blessing in my life. Certainly I had friends who would have been glad to do this for me, but I simply did not have the courage to ask them. When we experience a loss, our self-confidence is brutally beaten down, and our emotional bank accounts are totally overdrawn, so things that would ordinarily be easy become insurmountable tasks.

Kathy (Morrison) Ditlevson said this when her husband, Mitch, died, "It would have been so helpful if, during the first two months, I would have had offers of someone to call and ask me what I needed at the grocery store. I hardly had the energy the first several weeks to even go out and buy a gallon of milk."

Provide Lawn and Home Care
Roy Parnell shared what his neighbors did: "With both of us being physically hindered with our respective illnesses, my scleroderma and my wife's cancer, the practical challenge of keeping our beautiful lawn mowed and edged was, to say the least, difficult. We were overwhelmed with a gesture from our neighbors when we were told they had 'purchased' four summer months of professional lawn care service for our home. In addition, we've had any number of home chores, such as gutter cleaning, leaf raking, and bark spreading done by these dear community neighbors . . . all facilitated and coordinated by just one individual in the neighborhood, who we really didn't even know, who heard about our situation and took charge in facilitating and coordinating this incredible help in our time of need. Perhaps some caring people can't change the world, but they have impacted the lives of two physically challenged people in an incredible, tangible way."

Share Your Time and Notify Others for Them
Deb Haggerty of Orlando, Florida, expressed what she *wished* people had done for her: "When I had my surgeries in 2000, first the mastectomy and then the hysterectomy, several of my friends brought us dinners. While the food was greatly appreciated, what

I really would have liked was company—just to come and be with me. Roy had to travel and, after Mom went back home, it got lonely. It's hard to ask people to come and share time, but that would have been a blessing. The other thing I wished someone had offered was to notify my friends who were *not* on e-mail. With both our dads going home in 1999 and the cancer, the last thing I wanted to do was a holiday letter. I *still* haven't let some of my 'not yet on the Internet' friends know what happened. Someone offering to jot folks a note would have been priceless."

Give Gift Certificates for Dinners Out

Lori Kwasniewski's mother does not cook very much, so when her father died, friends who knew gave her mother gift certificates to local restaurants. They not only encouraged her to eat right, but it also provided a way to get her out of the house. She also said that one of the things that meant the most to her mother was when friends called her for lunch dates since she always had lunch with her husband.

Help Them Learn to Laugh Again

"Have fun! Because someone has died, life does not stop. It is perfectly okay and healing to have uproarious times of laughter mingled with the tears. Don't change the way you treated the person before. Begin to talk a bit about the future when they are ready. Share the grief, share the load, share the tears, share the laughter," says Debbie Preuss of British Columbia.

Lori Kwasniewski from Watertown, South Dakota, shared, "Everybody brings the ham, buns, salads, paper goods. One thing that we received and enjoyed because it was fun was a twelve-pack of beer, wine coolers, and pretzels. Since then, I have also brought this 'care package' to friends who have lost a parent!"

Patt Schwab from Seattle, Washington, shared this humorous story in what could be a not-so-humorous situation:

> Two weeks before Thanksgiving my dad called. He said my eighty-four-year-old mom wanted me to come home that weekend because she was dying and the priest was coming the next day to perform the last sacrament for her!

This was a shock, since I had talked to her just a few days before and she had only complained of a stomachache. I asked if she was in the hospital. Dad said no, but he was waiting for the doctor to call. He told me to check in the next afternoon.

When I called the next day, my mom answered. "Are you dying?" I asked. "No, it's hardly worth it," she sighed. She then complained about how the priest was twenty-five minutes late and only spent five minutes performing what should have been a more impressive ceremony. "After all," she said, "it *is* the last sacrament. I thought there would be a lot more to it. Not only that, the host was stale—you'd think when it's your last holy communion, the least a priest could provide would be a fresh host!"

She went on to say, "He is actually a nice guy and probably just needs a little feedback. I'll have to talk to him the next time I see him at Mass."

I agreed, "You're right. He probably doesn't get much feedback from the parishioners he performs the last rites for! Let me talk to my dad!"

Long story short, her salt levels were too low which apparently causes a kind of dementia. Since she already has some dementia, it made it much worse. I gave my presentations and got home a week later to find her on her feet, and, though frail, once more, the "salt of the earth." And, yes, she did give a rather surprised priest some feedback!

Care for the Memorial Spot

One of the most thoughtful and touching gifts I have ever received has been the graciousness of Lonnie Lee Bone to care for Charlie and Gavin's graves since my move to Florida. Although I know that "they" are not really there, it was devastating for me to leave their memory places so far away, especially knowing that I would only get back a time or two a year. My precious friend has made it her gift to regularly go to the cemetery and make sure things are neat. I also know that she takes plants and flowers often. My heart is at peace, knowing that their final resting place is being cared for by loving hands.

Help Them with Car Maintenance

Several months after Charlie died, I was invited to lunch by my longtime friend, Shannon Johnston. We left my car (Charlie's Mercury Marquis which my children call "the Grandpa mobile!") at her place and drove in hers. While I was gone, her husband, Ken, took the car to a station, had the oil checked and changed, the tires rotated, and a general tune-up. He even had it washed for me and filled the gas tank! Little did he know that I had never bought nor had to take care of a car—Charlie always did that—so I had no idea what needed to be done. Not only was I surprised and deeply touched by his kindness, but I was so grateful for a friend to help me learn those practical things.

Help with Home Maintenance

I was a blessed woman! Charlie took care of the finances, the car, and all the home maintenance, so I could be free to concentrate on my family and later on my business. When he died, I knew very little about any of those things. (One bit of advice to all of you is *not* to be too busy to learn about your personal situation before you are forced to!)

One of the best things anyone did for me after his death was to teach me what I needed to know to be safe in my home in Illinois. A dear friend from college days, Bud Verdi, came one weekend and literally gave me a tour of my house. He showed me where and how to shut off the gas and the water, how to clean the filters in my furnace, and what maintenance checks I needed to do regularly. He even had me write things down in a schedule so I would remember them. Best of all, he was patient with me and did not make me feel stupid!

Ruth Gagnon from Toronto, Canada, lost her young husband in a car accident last year. She says, "When my husband, Peter, was killed, I lost so much in a split second. I could not even have imagined the significance of all he did for my sons and me. Even though he was gone, the never-ending "honey-do" list still existed. For the most part, I could handle things, and my sons were a great help. Some of the time I could even hire help to accomplish a task. However, it was for those annoying little things that I couldn't handle that I wish a handy man could have offered help. Like all of us who are grieving, I hate asking."

Offer Help with Work and Personal Situations

Jim Feldman, a professional colleague whom I really did not know, made the following, heartfelt offer:

> I wept when I read your memo about Charlie's illness and your daughter's upcoming wedding. As you may know, I lost my wife to cancer sometime ago. It brought back too many of the pains and struggles we experienced. Please count on me for anything you need. I would be happy to do a presentation or two and of course give you the money. I would be happy to donate some airline tickets, hotel stays, etc. if that helps in any way. If you need anything for the wedding, a photographer, someone to drive folks around, hotel rooms, just let me know. I am single. I do not have to worry about a family so I can spend more time or effort on your behalf than perhaps others can. I am close to a lot of doctors here in Chicago and would be pleased to introduce you to them at any time. Northwestern, University of Chicago (I am on the Cancer Research Board), Rush are all long time associates. I was on the Board for Y-ME national organization for breast cancer and know many of the oncologists here in the city. While we really do not know each other, I want you to know that I have been there. I know what a helping hand is worth, and I want to extend it to you in any manner or fashion that I can. If there is anything, no matter how large or small, please do not hesitate to ask. I am here for you. I will pray for you.

His offer meant a great deal to me for the several reasons. First, it touched me deeply that he did not even know me well and yet made such generous offers. Second, it touched my heart with compassion for his loss. And finally, I was overwhelmed at the specifics of his offer because it made it easier for me to actually accept his help.

As a result of this offer, Jim truly gave me one of the most precious gifts I have ever received and one I will never forget! The Monday before Charlie died, I was presenting in Vermont and was planning to go on to speak in Canada the day after. That Monday afternoon I received a message from Charlie's brother that I should come home immediately. Since Jim had told me that any time I had a need, he would be willing to help, I knew I could ask him. Not only did he do the session in Canada at the last minute, but he also sent me *all* the money. The most amazing thing of all was that Charlie went to heaven at *exactly* the time Jim was speaking. All I could think of was that without Jim's help, I could have missed that precious moment of being by Charlie's side when he left this earth.

5. Remember the Children

Don't forget about me! When the funeral is over—I still grieve. When you see me, ask how I am doing. I know my mom lost her husband, and you ask how she is. I lost my dad, my only dad, my best friend. Ask me how I am doing too. Let me talk about my dad. Don't be afraid when I talk about him and try to change the subject. Don't be afraid to share what you remember about him too.
 —Lori Kwasniewski

The most important gift you can give your children at this time is the feeling that life continues despite the pain. Death, "the loss of innocence," can either lead you to the edge of the abyss and threaten your existence with meaninglessness and futility, or you will start to build the bridge that spans the chasm with things of life that still count—memory, family, friendship, love.
 —Rabbi Earl Grollman, *Talking about Death*

When a parent or grandparent dies, we often think of the spouse but sometimes forget the children. They grieve in their own way and need support too, and often that support must come from others because the surviving spouse is so immersed in their own grieving that they have nothing left to give the child. The most important message is that kids want to know that somehow the family is going to make it through this hard time and that there are friends and family to support them.

Jean Becker writes so poignantly about a child's grief and how others might have helped:

> I was just six years old when my mother died of pneumonia on Pearl Harbor Day, December 7, 1941. Those were the days before penicillin so there was nothing that could save her. I was

the second oldest of four sisters and an infant brother. We were whisked off by our father to another city to the home of one of my mother's sisters.

The loss of my mother was compounded as our father abandoned us, and our aunts and uncles divided us among themselves, separating us from our siblings. I wasn't told until days later that my mother had died. I was naked in the bathtub when my aunt scolded me for crying and told me to stop or I would be left alone there while they went to the grocery store. I wish she hadn't taken her anger out on me when she said, "Your mother would still be alive if your father had called for an ambulance sooner."

I wasn't allowed to go to the funeral or any of the gatherings arranged to provide comfort, so there was no human touch from mourning friends or relatives who visited the funeral home. There were no words of comfort for me from the clergy or sounds of familiar hymns to unleash free-flowing tears to bathe my grief. Notes of solace delivered by the mailman were not addressed to me. I couldn't even hold on to my teddy bear because it had been left behind.

I wish someone, anyone, would have held me for a few minutes and told me that it must hurt a lot to lose a mother. Just acknowledge that it was a devastating situation for me. Let me feel the grief and express it in tears while feeling comfort in the arms of another human being. Let me rest from the hardship for just a few minutes.

If no one acknowledges this at the time of loss or within the year, it seems that it may never happen because the opportunities become so rare as life speeds by. There is focus on education, career, marriage, and raising a family and still no one even thinks to acknowledge this great loss.

It finally happened for me when I was forty-one years old and it took a psychiatrist to touch my trembling hand and offer his condolence. "I wish I could bring your mother back to you. If I could, you know I would do that for you. But I can't. I am so sorry."

I wish someone, anyone, would have insisted that my sisters and baby brother could stay together. I wish someone, anyone, would have stepped forward to become my advocate. I wish I had not been abandoned again into an orphan home. I felt there was no one to love me.

I wish I could have worn a symbol or pin that would let people know that my mother had died, so she would not die over and over, every time the teacher said, "Take this note home to your mother" or when a someone else's mother would say, "Ask your mother if you can play after school today." There are countless times when mothers are referred to almost every day. All through my growing up years, my mother died a thousand times.

© Jean Becker. Reprinted with permission.

Tell the Children the Truth about What Happened

Many times parents feel that they should not show their emotions or talk about the death of a family member around young children. However, again and again the research has shown that in later years those children have many scars because of the lack of communication. When the loss is sudden and it is not explained to them, they can feel as if they have been the cause, and at the very least they are confused and angry, yet they have no one to talk to about it. And sometimes they are even afraid that they, too, might simply die one day for no reason.

Not only do children understand much more than we give them credit for, but they are also very resilient. It is best to tell them the truth to the extent that they can understand at their age level, and then remember that you will need to share the story with them many times as they grow up, since their understanding will differ with their maturity level. If they are not told the truth about what has happened, they may hear it from friends or people in your community, and that would be even harder to bear. They need to be allowed to grieve in their own way, so creating honest and open communication, even though it may be difficult for the parent or loved one, is critical at this time. When children see adults grieving, then they know it is all right for them to grieve too.

Help Them Express Their Anger

Kathy (Morrison) Ditlevson shares how a caring person helped her daughter when her husband died of massive brain injury in a bicycling accident:

My daughter, Jessica, was very angry at the loss of her father. She was angry with God, the doctors, even her dad, and everyone in between. She kept saying, "I am so angry . . . I wish I could break something—I just want to break something!" Her youth group minister's wife, Paula, heard her say this, so Paula purchased some inexpensive, breakable dishes and gave her the box at church one Sunday morning. Paula told Jessica that, when she was ready, to go somewhere and break the dishes. A few weeks after her dad's death, Jessica went to the warehouse of another friend of ours and threw each dish against the wall, as well as the broken pieces. She felt better when she came home that evening.

There is no rhyme nor reason to how we sometimes process grief, but these dishes were such a creative gift to my daughter. It gave her permission to express her anger in a constructive way without hurting herself or others. She continued to deal with her anger over a period of months, but that particular evening gave her some relief from the intensity of it.

Mark Camacho writes about what he learned that would have helped his daughter when her mother died:

I tried to pull my daughter out of her great sadness at eleven years old, just months after her mom died, by encouraging her to embrace the love and light of a new life, a new beginning, and all that is good and abundant—to embrace life and not get buried in despair and loss. It's only recently, now that Lauren is fifteen, that I understand her anger toward me. Although it occurred on many levels, one area is certain. She resented me for not allowing her to live in anguish and pain. She *needed* to feel that place. She needed to scream out to God and experience that loss. I tried so hard to protect her from the pain, but instead she interpreted my actions as unsympathetic toward her mother. She felt like I did not share in her despair, that I didn't care. She felt all alone. I thought I was doing the right thing by speaking of love, encouragement, God's divine plan. She just wanted to be sad. I needed to allow that until she was ready for something different.

Plant Marigolds
Elissa Ecker shares how a teacher handled a parent's death with the children in the class in a very special way that focused on good memories:

A dear friend of mine died in the spring after a valiant, courageous and two-and-a-half-year fight with breast cancer. She had just turned thirty-nine and had two sons. The youngest child was in kindergarten, and the other child was in my daughter's third grade class. When my friend died, the middle school religion teacher (they go to a parochial school), met with both third grade classes to discuss what had happened and to give the children an opportunity to talk about their feelings and beliefs . . . an opportunity to share their thoughts about the boys and my friend. All the children knew my friend because she was a very active parent and parishioner.

The teacher gave each child a packet of marigold seeds and told them to plant them in their yards. By doing this, God would give us a constant reminder this summer and fall of my friend and we would be able to remember all the wonderful things she had done. We are still enjoying our marigolds this summer. Each time we look at the flowers we remember to say a little prayer for my friend, her husband, and her boys.

I think this is an excellent idea to share with children who have lost someone. The flowers keep the flow of communication of this very difficult topic open. Less than two weeks ago, my daughter was thinking about the boys and she asked me, "What will happen to the boys if Mr. 'M.' dies?" This had apparently been bothering her, and we went into a long conversation about what would happen if something happened to my husband and me. I strongly believe the constant beauty of the marigolds is a blessing.

Give Them a Teddy Bear

Roy Saunderson tells of what one nurse did to bring him lifelong comfort: "My mother died giving birth to me in the mid-1950s. I am sure this was hard on the hospital staff as well as on my dear dad who grieved the loss of his sweetheart. Still in my possession, and in fact on my bedside table in a plastic see-through container, is the little teddy bear given to me by a concerned nurse who must have cared for me before my dad could muster up the courage to bring me home. 'Teddy' is a little threadbare now, but he is a constant daily reminder when I wake up to think about how I can lighten someone's day as one unknown nurse did for me."

In many places, a teddy bear has come to be a symbol of love and comfort. I have read that the highway patrolmen in the State of Minnesota carry teddy bears in the trunks of their cars to give to children who have been traumatized in an accident.

Sometimes as adults we need them too! Just after Charlie's first surgery when we thought he was going to be fine, we realized a lifelong dream of his—to have a little place in Florida. He was a golfer and I am a swimmer, so to be close to water was a blessing for us both. In fact, we spent the last two months of his life in our new little villa on Siesta Key.

Several weeks after we had arrived at the villa, we received a package from Curt Hansen. He wrote to Charlie:

> As Barbara knows, I have not had the fortunate opportunity to meet either one of you. However, I must tell you that my life has changed since I first faxed Barbara a note several months ago. Since that first fax, I have developed a deeper appreciation for the simpler things in life and a time to refocus my life on family, friends, and others. Charlie, your "temporary challenge" has taught me so much by your just being you and hearing all the wonderful things people have told me about you, and I thank you from my heart.
>
> Your indirect message to me was "Curt, listen to your heart and react to the spirit of God within you." What a difference it has made in my relationships with friends and family. Your inspiration has renewed the lost enthusiasm and spirit I used to have!
>
> Enclosed you will find two bears. The bears are there to remind both of you that others are praying for you and thinking of you. Even when we cannot be there in person, we can always be with you in your hearts. May you both continue to know God's love in everything you feel, see, and do.

After Charlie died, I decided that first winter to work from our little place in Florida. That first trip back to the villa was a heart-rending one for me since that had been where Charlie and I had had our last happy times. My longtime friend, Shannon Johnston, picked me up at the airport that day and then drove me to the villa. She had offered to stay overnight with me that first night; however, I knew I had to face being alone, so I decided not to accept her offer. Just before she left, she gave me a huge, soft stuffed dog. She said, "This can be your 'Charlie' dog. He can sleep with you, and you can hug him anytime you are lonely." Since I had not slept alone for nearly thirty-four years, you cannot imagine what a comfort my "Charlie" dog was! To this day, he resides in my bedroom, and I often reach over for a big, comforting hug.

Spend Time with the Children, Take Them Places, and Talk with Them

Kathy (Morrison) Ditlevson also talked about her boys and what she wished had happened more: "Especially during the first several months after Mitch died, it was so helpful when families from the church would call and offer to pick up my boys and take them somewhere. It would have been helpful if that offer had come more often, and even eighteen months after Mitch's death, if the offer would still come. My boys need to still be around Christian men as role models."

Debbie Preuss offers this advice: "If there are small children, take them out for a while. Children grieve in spurts, not like adults. Let them know it is okay to talk about the deceased person. Let the kids ask questions—you don't have to know all the answers. Just asking is therapeutic, and you can research answers you don't know and share with them at a later time. Pray with the children. Let them pray too. Listen to what they're not saying. Above all, don't make promises to them that you can't keep."

A woman shared what she appreciated after her husband died: "Other thoughtful things are when people remember the kids' birthdays and bring them gifts. I found that I really didn't care about myself so much, but my children really needed the attention and I wasn't up to giving it, so any little thoughtful gift or outing was really appreciated. A few men in my church had a heart for my son with having six sisters, so they would take him fishing or hunting, you know, all the 'guy' things."

Help Them Remember the Loved One

Experts suggest that you invite children to suggest ways to remember lost ones, especially during the holidays. Don't "protect" them by leaving them out of remembrance rituals.

Denise White from Michigan tells about what they did to help their son's little boy remember him long after his death:

At the time of his passing, Shawn's only son, Mavrick, was just three years old. The entire family was grief-stricken and concerned about Mavrick remembering his dad. At the services, we passed out 5" x 8" cards beautifully engraved with the words, "A Letter to Mavrick." Family and friends were asked to share a note about Shawn that would be passed on to Mavrick. The response was overwhelming. It still to this day touches my heart to think about how wonderful so many people were to us during that time and how loved our son was. These cards turned out to be a source of comfort to our whole family.

On the date of Shawn's passing, March 17, wherever the family is, they pause and light a candle to show that his light still shines for us. Former classmates bring personal keepsakes of Shawn to the gravesite for Mavrick. Each March 17, we receive e-mail messages from across the country from many of them.

Sandy Donaldson creates a memory box: "When a child loses a parent or grandparent, I buy a beautiful box or jar and put the name of the loved one on the top. I cut up small pieces of paper (about thirty) and include directions to the child to write as many fun memories as they can of their lost one—one memory on each slip of paper. Then I direct them to take them out one at a time, whenever they miss their loved one. I like this since so many times children are ignored as people do not know what to say to them, but they need comfort too."

Elaine Ingalls Hogg, the author of a book on death and bereavement for children, feels that many times children hide their feelings because they sense that the adults around them are not comfortable talking with them. She relates the following incidents:

Recently during an Authors in the School visit, a grade-three child stopped me in the hall. "Mrs. Hogg, I have something to tell you." Earlier in the morning, she had attended my presentation as a visiting author. On the display table I'd arranged my early scribbles, rewrites, letters to and from the editor, and the finished book, *Remembering Honey,* an award-winning picture book to help young children discuss their feelings of loss. We had not read that particular story, but it was among the books on display.

Now the teacher was hustling the class out for recess. The line started to move toward the playground. I smiled at the small round face and wished we had more time. Suddenly the girl broke out of line and gave me a quick hug. "I have someone I remember too," she whispered. "It's my mom. She moved away two years ago." Before I could say anything, the child ran back to the end of the line. All I could do was smile and wave.

This incident confirmed my growing belief: Children need an opportunity to express their grief, for this was not the first time something like this had happened. In September when my day was finished after another school visit, I was packing up to go home. "Elaine, wait!" The grade-one teacher came rushing down the hall. "I have something to show you."

Earlier in the day, in my role as visiting author, I'd been reading to the students in her classroom. My book is not an easy story to read to young students as it talks about death and bereavement. During my time in the class, one student asked me, "Why did you write such a sad book?" My answer was, "Sometimes sad things happen, and I want boys and girls like you to know it is okay to be sad. But I also want you to know there are people who love you and want to help you when you feel this way." I went on to explain children should be encouraged to talk about their feelings and perhaps make a memory box or memory shelf. Now the teacher was showing me a decorated shoebox that six-year-old Kaitlin had made over the noon hour.

Inside her shoebox Kaitlin had placed fish filters and fish food in memory of her three dead gold fish. But that wasn't all; beside the fish food was a picture of a puppy that I later learned was her grandfather's dog and a picture of her "Poppy," as she called her grandfather. Even more moving was the poem she wrote expressing a mature awareness of the cycle of life. It read, "In the 'fusor I will be the onely one left in my famlie."

Last week a grade-one teacher advised me she had spent an hour listening to her students' stories of loss after reading *Remembering Honey* to the children. She said, "The children told me of their private grieving; they shared things they have never told anyone else."

I often encourage them to write about their feelings. One small boy never spoke about the fact that he was still missing his friend until the day four years later when he was invited to write a story about someone special in his life. He wrote about the night he was walking along the highway with his friend. He was six when a car hit his friend who was walking beside him. "He never came back," he wrote. "They told me he was in the hospital, but he never came back. Now I know he's dead." Young children may not be able to write, but many love to draw and color. Take time to discuss their drawings and stories. It's amazing what they will tell you if they think you are willing to spend time with them and really listen!

©Elaine Ingalls Hogg. Reprinted with permission

Search for Books and Videos That Will Help the Children Understand

A Canadian friend suggests this: "If a loved one is ill and there are children to be cared for, offer to take them and minister to them. Give them a fun-filled day or a quiet day, just a special time when the children can speak about their own grief. Children grieve too. Go to your local Christian bookstore and investigate the materials (videos and books) that will help a little one understand and grow in their own faith. Care enough to pray with us, whether we be adult or children. Let us know in so doing that you care enough about us to usher us into the presence of a loving God."

6. Be the One to Reach Out

A broken heart cries out, "See me!" The grieving feel invisible.
—Tom Ehrich, "On a Journey"

An odd by-product of my loss is that I'm aware of being an embarrassment to everyone I meet. . . . Perhaps the bereaved ought to be isolated in special settlements like lepers.
—C. S. Lewis, *A Grief Observed*

I share with you the agony of your grief,
The anguish of your heart finds echo in my own.
I know I cannot enter all you feel
Nor bear with you the burden of your pain;
I can but offer what my love does give:
The strength of caring.
The warmth of one who seeks to understand,
The silent storm swept barrenness of so great a loss.
This I do in quiet ways
That on your lonely path
You may not walk alone.
—Howard Thurman, *Meditations of the Heart*

One of the most important things I have learned about helping someone in the midst of grieving is *don't wait* for them to ask for help. Don't ask, "What can I do?" because they either won't know or they won't feel comfortable asking. Their emotional bank account is completely overdrawn, and they don't even have the energy to think what they might need. *Just do it!*

Share Food and Comforting Words, Call Regularly

Jan Krouskop from South Carolina shared things that meant a lot to her:

> When my dad passed away, I was blessed with many kind gestures that really helped.
>
> 1. My best friend immediately came over laden with food. She didn't ask if I wanted it or needed it—but just brought over ham, fruit, rolls, and salad. She also sat with me until my sister arrived from out of town just making small talk and letting me talk about Dad. When the rest of the family arrived, she simply disappeared.
>
> 2. A neighbor, realizing that I had a house full of family staying over, brought breakfast the morning of the funeral. It was quite nice—fresh fruit, bagels, pastries, etc.
>
> 3. My pastor, knowing that I was the oldest child in the family and the one who usually holds everyone else up, sent me a touching e-mail, giving me permission to grieve and cry—and included comforting Bible passages. I read this in the middle of the night when I couldn't sleep, and it was like having a hand to hold in the darkness.
>
> 4. A friend literally called me daily for many weeks to see how I was—and having lost a parent herself, she assured me when I thought I would never think straight again or stop crying.

Send Flowers

Kathy (Morrison) Ditlevson tells how much flowers meant to her: "Kathy and Joe Lamancusa sent me flowers several weeks after my husband died. They were so bright and cheery and meant so much to me. It was so nice to know that someone was still thinking about me and praying for me. I knew that God loved me through this kind expression of love. Since then, I have passed the gift on. When my mother-in-law was dying, I sent flowers to her. She absolutely loved looking at them. When they took her to the hospital, she took those flowers with her and they were in her room when she died."

Debbie Preuss also suggests that you wait to send flowers until at least a month after the service when everyone else has gone back to their normal lives. She cautions you to write it on your calendar, though, so you won't forget. Like Kathy, she feels that the receiver will appreciate them much more after the flurry of the funeral.

I appreciated especially the people who sent me plants when Charlie died because these can go on and on as reminders of people's love. I gave a plant to each of our children to take home after the funeral, and they still have them today! I will never forget one plant that came from Charlie's best golfing buddies—the plant was surrounded by plastic golf balls. (To this day whenever I am able to go to his graveside, I find golf balls in the planter there!) When I moved from Chicago to Florida two years ago, I could not take one of the larger plants from Charlie's service, so I gave it to Pam Burks, a dear friend who lives in Indiana. She tells me that she thinks of Charlie each time she waters it!

The Importance of Touch

When Karen Rowinsky lost her young husband, Max, she, like all of us who are grieving, desperately missed touch:

> After Max died, the loneliness was pervasive. My heart had a void no one but Max could fill. My body, however, ached for human touch, Max's for sure, but at some point, anyone's. In those first days when people were around, I received plenty of hugs, but after my friends went back to their everyday lives, the hugs stopped. My skin hurt from the lack of touch. I tried a massage therapist, but it felt too intimate and I ended up crying through it.
>
> Then a couple, Leslie and Tim, who were good friends with both Max and me, took me out to dinner. We came back to the house and I was talking with them about how hard it was not to cuddle, when Tim just held out his arms. Without saying anything, I moved over to the couch next to him and he just held me. It was not sexual, just comforting. We sat there and continued the conversation for a while and I just snuggled in his arms. I cried a little but mostly tried to make myself savor the feeling. After that, whenever I was with Leslie and Tim, I got some cuddling. I so appreciated the generosity of Leslie in knowing why I needed this and being willing to share. Tim is not usually a demonstrative person, yet what he gave me during that time showed me how much he cared about me and Max.

Robin Maynard says this, "I wish people would just hold out their arms and provide a silent hug, instead of avoiding someone in grief because they don't know what to say."

Invite Them to Do Things with You

One of the hardest things for me when my husband died was that I was no longer a part of a "couple." Let's face it, it is a couple's world, and I had been part of a couple my whole adult life. Now all of a sudden I was a single person. What I discovered was that I was no longer being included in "couples" gatherings, partly I think, because people did not want to make me feel uncomfortable or lonely. However, my advice to you is to *always* invite the bereaved person. Let her or him make the choice about whether to come or not. Even though there would have been many times I would not have attended a party or function, leaving me out just increased my loneliness.

Also, don't forget that a divorce is nearly like a death, and sometimes even harder since the other person is still alive. The person who is suddenly alone can feel just as lonely, and sometimes perhaps even more so because they may feel society is judging them or that in some way they have failed. They are grieving, too, for a lost life, so they need the same love and caring as someone whose spouse has died.

A grieving person might warn the host ahead of time about the possibility of leaving without a good-bye if he or she becomes too uncomfortable. One bereaved woman even carried a pre-written letter in her pocket explaining why she had to leave in a rush and thanking the host. Even if people never use the letter, it makes them more comfortable to attend social events because they have a polite "out." These are good suggestions to give when you invite a hurting person who may be reluctant to come to a social gathering of some kind.

Valla Dana Fotiades shared ways friends ministered to her by including her in their plans: "In September, after John's death in May, Beth spotted me at church and made me promise to attend a play that a few women from our church were starring in. I did not feel like going. She said she knew that, but she would pick me up at 7:15. I went and enjoyed it. When I explained to another friend, Chris, how difficult Friday nights were, she suggested we make Friday night craft night. Now, we have been doing craft nights for many months and it is great to have something to look forward to on the weekends."

My dear friend, Karna Burkeen, whose husband died unexpectedly at a young age, decided that, she was going to handle two difficult times by including others who were lonely. Both on Super Bowl Sunday and New Years Eve, days that most grieving people spend home alone, she called all the widows she knew and visited with them over the telephone. Many of them were alone and lonely and admitted that, while they did not miss the football games, they did miss the socialization and appreciated the phone calls.

Remember the Caretaker

When Charlie was very ill, a dear friend from California, Carol Jo DeFore, gave me one of the most wonderful gifts I have ever received. She said that because she couldn't be there in person to help me, she was sending me a check to do something special "just for myself." She informed me that I was *not* to use it to pay medical bills or groceries or anything mundane—I was to go to a spa or buy something new or take a class, whatever would restore my soul. I cried and cried when I opened that envelope because I had been so busy taking care of Charlie, the rest of the family, and running a household and a business, that I had taken no thought of myself. The check was for a significant amount of money, and we were in a tight spot at that time, so it was overwhelming to think that I was *supposed* to do something just for me! In the end, I used it to pay for the booklets we had printed for Charlie's service, so it not only was special for me, but it also touched hundreds of other lives.

Just Be There—In Whatever Ways They Need You

Alyice Edrich of Sioux Falls, South Dakota, shares all the amazing ways people reached out and helped her in her loss:

> Six years ago, my daughter died in an untimely and stupid accident. I was beside myself with grief, anger, guilt, and shame. It was a devastation like none I had ever experienced before and something I could not lightly get over. I couldn't lift a finger to care for my other children, to take care of funeral arrangements, to offer support to my spouse, or to care for myself. It was as if, for a time, I too had died.
>
> The most important thing I needed when I suffered my loss, was time to "just grieve." I needed time to do nothing more than cry and deal with the great loss I had been faced with. I couldn't think about anything else but what I had lost and what would never be.

Outside my home, life was still going on and I couldn't bear facing that. It made me angrier than I had ever been in my life. I didn't know how to function and I didn't understand how life could just go on. I wanted to give up on life, I wanted others to feel what I felt, and I didn't want to be along in this pain—and yet, I felt all alone.

Then the care packages arrived. My church, my town, and several family members came to my aid. Without asking, they reached out to me in unexpected and much needed ways. I will never forget their kindness or their compassion. They were a true testament of God's abiding grace.

The truth is: Grieving people do not know to ask for help. They can't think past the pain. They need someone to step up and just do—do whatever needs to be done, no questions asked.

The following is only the tip of the iceberg when it comes to the remarkable amount of support I received after my daughter passed away. And every single bit of it has allowed me to heal and move forward:

1. Small groups within my church got together and provided dinners and a nightly prayer for my family for an entire two months.

2. My pastor, with the help of my mother and sister-in-law, took care of all the funeral arrangements.

3. My mother came to live with us for a few months, taking care of the home, shopping, paying bills, and caring for my children.

4. My sister took my children the first week, to help them when I couldn't.

5. A friend came every Friday to take my children to the park while another picked them up every day and took them to school for six entire months.

6. One lady took it upon herself to send anonymous letters and hand-made cards of encouragement and hope while strangers from all over would send cards of sympathy and empathy. Oh, how I looked forward to those cards!

7. My other sister came from Missouri. She was the only one who could get me to eat, after two days of not eating.

8. A friend came, every other day, just to sit on my bed and watch movies with me. She never offered advice, and never told me it was time to move on. She just sat there letting me know that if I needed someone to reach out to, she was there.

9. My pastor came every day for the first few weeks, just to check in on us. He would remind me that God loved us and that he was praying for us. He never said much, but if I started to look better, he would mention it. I remember the day he said, "It looks as though a dark cloud as been removed from over your head." It was then that I realized I was moving on with my grief and accepting my loss.

10. A local counselor would come to our home every day to listen and get us to talk about our loss and what we were feeling. After a while, when he felt we were strong enough, he asked us to meet him once a week in his office.

11. One lady left a framed picture of Jesus holding a baby, just to show she cared while another made an artificial flower arrangement. She came with the flowers and simply said, "I heard about your loss. I just had to do something and I didn't know what to do since I don't know you. But my daughter does, and so I made you this." I still have the arrangement as a reminder that God's love abounds in all of us.

12. An anonymous person left a note on my door, which said that flowers had been planted in the park behind my house, in remembrance of my child.

13. A local author and her husband came and sat with us when she heard. She gave us a copy of her book which dealt with grief and invited us to a local grief support group.

14. A local singer gave me a plaque that says, "God will mend your heart, if you give him all the pieces." I have that plaque displayed. To this day, it reminds me when things get tough, that I haven't given God all the pieces.

15. And finally, I received a lot of forgiveness and compassion. In my grief, I was angry and misdirected that anger at many loved ones, strangers, and friends. They have all since accepted my apologies and extended their hands of forgiveness by simply stating, "I understand you were grieving."

Years later, I have improved and grown in my grief, but there are still moments when I simply feel a deep sense of loss and loneliness over the loss of my daughter. It is then that I withdraw from my loved ones, and it is then that they have learned to push back and reach out. What a great comfort it is to still be able to talk about the child I loved, to remember the good times, and to be allowed to still share the pain her loss has left on my life.

©Alyice Edrich. Reprinted with permission.

Your Presence Means the Most

Jane Jones of Cedar Rapids, Iowa, shares a sweet story about two levels of reaching out:

My parents have fed their two garbage men breakfast every Friday for years. A wrapped egg sandwich and coffee is placed outside their back door, and these men are accustomed to this and have built a relationship with my parents.

My father passed away in Baltimore on Wednesday, March 24, 2002. Even on the day of his memorial service that Friday, my mother put out the usual breakfast for their friends. Since they did not know about my dad's death, she watched for them to tell them. They were very upset to hear about Dad and expressed their desire to attend the service except that they were not dressed appropriately. My mother told them she would love to have them come and that they looked just fine.

While we were waiting at the church, my sister and I saw the garbage truck pull up right behind the hearse. My sister commented that she hoped they would put Dad in the right vehicle! (How often we need to have a sense of humor in difficult situations.)

The two garbage men in their regular work uniforms were among the five hundred people who attended Dad's memorial service. What a contrast to find Senator Mikalsky of Baltimore was in line right behind them! I can assure you that it meant just as much to me and my mom to have the garbage men present as Maryland's excellent U.S. senator.

This story serves as a testimony of how to treat people and to show respect for everyone, regardless of their station in life. I will always cherish the memory of my parents' special friends, the garbage men!

7. Use Your Unique Talents

There's a formula Chris and I used all the time. When you *least* feel like it, do something for someone else. You forget about your own situation. It gives you a purpose, as opposed to being sorrowful and lonely. It makes me feel better when things are too hard for me.
—Dana Reeve, widowed wife of Christopher Reeve

Use your talent, use it every way possible. . . . Spend it lavishly like a millionaire intent on going broke.
—Brendan Francis Behan

Comfort and prosperity have never enriched the world as adversity has done. Out of pain and problems have come the sweetest songs, the most poignant poems, the most gripping stories. Out of suffering and tears have come the greatest spirits and the most blessed lives.
—Billy Graham

When you want to help a friend who is grieving, it is best to do something that feels comfortable for you. If you can find a way to use your own special interests and talents to help another person, you will be giving them a very special gift of caring.

Create a "Grieving Box"
A woman from Columbus, Ohio, who loves crafts has been sending people who have lost someone a "grieving box" where they can put things to remember them, such as pictures, personal items, etc. This is not a business but just her special way of helping people deal with the loss.

Shine Their Shoes

Another man shared that when he hears of a loss in a family, he goes to their home with his shoeshine kit. When they answer the door, he tells them to show him where their bedroom is and then to go on about their business. He proceeds to shine all the shoes in the closet! He says it is something he is good at and something that he can offer to help the grieving family.

Create a Talk about the Person to Share with Others or Start a Scholarship

Scott Marcus, who is now an inspirational professional speaker from Eureka, California, told me, "When my mother passed away suddenly, I did two things that helped a great deal: 1) I wrote a speech and entered it in a Toastmasters contest to help spread who she was, and 2) My sister and I started a scholarship through a nonprofit foundation to help aspiring writers. It is the most comforting thing I have ever done, and it can be started very inexpensively. It helps keep her alive on another level."

Make Something from the Loved One's Clothing

When Kathy (Morrison) Ditlevson's husband died from a bicycling accident, a dear friend offered to use her special skills to bring comfort to the family:

> Kathy Lamancusa asked me a few weeks after my husband, Mitch, died if my children and I would allow her to make quilts for each one of us out of Mitchell's clothing. I was thrilled at the offer, especially because it gave me such relief in knowing that I didn't have to give his clothes away. As the weeks went by, I slowly removed his socks from the drawer, his shirts and pants from the closet, and they all went upstairs into the attic.
>
> Several months later, Kathy came to my home. My three children and I removed the clothes from the attic and chose which item of clothing we each wanted in our quilt. It was a process that continued to help all of us heal, especially as we shared some stories in the room about why some of the clothing we chose meant something to us. There was laughter and some tears and such relief in knowing that his clothes were something we could hold on to, along with the wonderful, fun, and sweet memories we have of him.

One of the chapters of Bereaved Parents of the USA assembled a quilt in memory of all their children. Each child was remembered on one 12" by 12" square, and the friend or parent could decorate it any way they chose. What a wonderful way to memorialize their children!

Someone else suggested cutting items of the loved one's clothing into small squares with pinking shears. Push them into a straw wreath with pins or an ice pick. These become a lovely memorial, and they could be made for many family members.

A person in Belleville, Illinois, makes "memory bears" from people's clothes. She uses wedding gowns, suits, fur coats, and other personal items of people who have died.

Make a Pillow from Their Ties

Roy Saunderson of London, Ontario, Canada, shared a precious idea when a man dies:

> After Irene's dad passed away, Irene signed up for her first class as a beginning quilter. One of the ladies who was in the class brought her sewing material in a bag that was clearly made up from men's ties. Irene commented on how lovely the bag was and learned that the ties belonged to her late husband. This sparked Irene's imagination to make something from her dad's ties for her mother. So, with permission, Irene collected up her dad's modest collection of ties and then quilted them into a pillow. Each tie tells a story, and Mom now treasures the pillow as it is placed on a chair in the living room.
>
> This past year a young couple we know experienced a serious tragedy. The husband, Mike Gillespe, was a well-loved teacher at an elementary school in London, Ontario, and died following the injuries from a car accident.
>
> Irene and two girlfriends have long had a monthly get together to talk, quilt, and share a lunch as they rotate from one another's homes. She remembered that Mike had hundreds of ties and that is no exaggeration! She approached her quilting buddies and asked how they would feel about making pillows up for Mike's wife, Chantelle, his four-year-old son, and for Mike's mother. They agreed this would be a wonderful idea.
>
> Just a couple of months after Mike's death and before anyone had thought about keeping or giving away Mike's clothes, Irene

asked Chantelle about the idea and whether she would accept them making these pillows. The idea was gratefully accepted.

So the pillows were made and Irene and each of her friends took care and thought as to which ties to select for each recipient. There were the thin ties of years gone by, the national sports team insignia ones, the Looney Toons and other cartoon characters, and the sentimental "I Love Daddy" emblazoned ties. All were individually selected and lovingly crafted into individual pillows. Mike's mom wrote a card after receiving her pillow saying how touched she and her husband were and how treasured the pillow was to them.

Build a Memorial Web Site

Robin Maynard shared that she *wished* someone had done this for her family members. If you have this talent, what a lasting and precious gift it would be! As you have read in this book, several people have done this to memorialize their friends and loved ones.

Create a Tribute to the Person

Debbie Preuss suggests that you use your own particular talents to create some sort of tribute to the person who has died. You may write a poem, put together a scrapbook, frame a photo of the person, write a letter, create a video collage, do a drawing, or anything else you can think of.

When Charlie died on a Wednesday afternoon, of course I could not sleep that night. In the wee hours of the morning, I decided that I needed to do something special that would touch many other people so I decided to create a memorial booklet to be handed out at his service on Saturday. I wrote a tribute to him titled, "Romantic Gifts," and then I included writings, poems, and letters that had meant a lot to both of us during the time he was ill. I also included a biography of Charlie. (You may view a copy of this booklet on my Web site at www.barbaraglanz.com in the "Family Life" section.)

The next day I got everyone in the family involved which provided a healthy project to focus on. My youngest daughter and two of her friends went through old photo albums (with much laughter and delight at the "old" styles of dress and hair!) for pictures, my other daughter and her husband formatted the booklet, and my son worked with my assistant on getting it to the printer. In just two days we had several hundred beautiful color copies of the booklet to share with others at the service. Many people have commented on how much this tribute meant to them and how many people they have shared it with.

Write a Poem

When Tom Burley's mother died, his friend and neighbor wrote a poem to remember her:

> Neighborhoods can be made or ruined by the influence of one set of neighbors. We are fortunate that God heard and answered my wife's sincere prayers when the house across the street went up for sale. Tom and Patsy Jacoy were God's answer to my wife's pleading. Soon after they moved in, we became fast friends. We take care of each other's children and get together often.
>
> Tom and Patsy stood beside us during the many months that my wife's mother, Serene D. Zurschmiede, fought ovarian cancer. In July of 2001, Serene went home to her Lord and Creator. A few days after her death, Tom and Patsy presented Linda, my better-half, and me with a Vine-Maple tree. Attached to the lovely tree was a poem written by Patsy:

> Are you surprised to see me?
> I'm surprised to be here too.
> I am here to keep a watchful eye
> on all you say and do
>
> Please find a place to put me
> a place where I can grow
> And when the wind blows on my leaves
> That's my whisper of, "I love you so."
>
> I will watch your very busy lives
> I will watch you work and play
> I will make sure the Lord's presence
> Is with you night and day
>
> Come to me for shelter from wind or sun or rain,
> Tell me all your stories of happiness, joy, or pain.
> I'm a shoulder you can cry on, a shoulder on which to lean
> From now until forever, I am the memory of Serene.
> —Patsy Jacoy, August 2001

To this day, that poem is hung in a prominent position in our home. It is a constant reminder of the most selfless of mothers, Serene, and the most thoughtful of friends, Tom and Patsy Jacoy.

Make a "Memory Book"

Kathie Hightower shares this idea of a gift for a grieving friend:

> A friend of mine who lost her only son said that one thing she wanted was for people to talk to her about him—to reminisce, to keep his memory alive—whereas most folks seemed afraid to bring his name up.
>
> I had the thought that a memory book might be a wonderful gift. It takes work. I did this for my mother's eightieth birthday and for my husband's promotion. I sent a photo album page to each friend (sneaked in and borrowed her address book!), asking for memories, photos, thoughts.
>
> This might also be a way to capture stories, especially from those who live too far to come to a funeral. It is something that can be treasured and returned to many times. A wonderful thing about these memory books is that the photos that arrive are usually photos the family has never seen as they were taken by others. These bring back all kinds of memories they may have forgotten.

Phyllis Landstrom writes about the scrapbooks she created for her family members: "Scrapbooking has become popular in Atlanta where I live. I found the most beautiful scrapbooks with a gardening theme that my mother would have loved. She always had a beautiful yard full of flowers . . . roses and iris's were her favorites. My sister Erica and I culled through stacks and stacks of photos. Her husband, Jay, works for Kodak, so he helped us get five reprints of each selected photo so that we could make six identical scrapbooks . . . one for each daughter and one for Dad! Each page in the scrapbook had a theme for interests that my mom had such as gardening, the Braves baseball team, square dancing, travel, cooking, family group outings, and boating. It helped us in our grieving to concentrate on the soul and essence of the person we loved. The scrapbooks turned out great, and we shared the finished product at the memorial service."

Write a Song

My precious friend, David Roth, wrote this song for all his friends who are going through difficult times:

> I can't say I know how you feel
> Wouldn't claim to know what you're going through
> But I know it's hard, so all I can do is be here for you
> I'll be here for you
>
> Sometimes I feel so lonely
> Is that the way that you're feeling now?
> Do you want to scream at the top of your lungs
> But you don't know how
>
> When you don't know what to do
> That's when I will be here for you
> I'll be here for you.
>
> I don't really have any answers
> And I don't always know what to do
> But if shoulders were meant to be leaned upon
> Then I'm putting one out here for you
> I will take up arms as your ally
> Any time or place that you need me to
> And I'll use these arms to embrace you
> And to hold you tight
> Through your darkest kind of night
>
> That's when I will be here
> I'll be here for you.
>   —David Roth
>   © 1987 David Roth, www.davidrothmusic.com

When my husband, Charlie, died, David flew to Western Springs to be there for his service, and on the way he wrote a beautiful song for Charlie. David was Charlie's favorite musician, and all through his chemo treatments, David's CDs were the only ones he listened to. David's precious tribute to him is one none of us in the family will ever forget.

Paint a Picture

Peter Hart from Montreal, Quebec, shared with me that when his mother died, his father surprised them all by reciting this poem:

Break, Break, Break
by Lord Alfred Tennyson

Break, break, break
On thy cold grey stones, O Sea!
And I would that my tongue could utter
The thoughts that arise in me.

O well for the fisherman's boy,
That he shouts with his sister at play!
O well for the sailor lad,
That he sings in his boat on the bay!

And the stately ships go on
To their haven under the hill;
But O for the touch of a vanished hand,
And the sound of a voice that is still!
Break, break, break
At the foot of thy crags, O Sea!
But the tender grace of a day that is dead
Will never come back to me.

Peter, who is an artist, was so touched by his father's words that he painted a lovely picture of an ocean scene for him which he titled, "Break, Break, Break." I feel blessed to have been given a framed print of this picture which carries such heartfelt meaning.

Write a Book

A speaker friend, Janie Jasin, CSP, tells about how she came to write her best-selling book:

My grief was overwhelming when my dad died of Alzheimer's complications and at the same time my mom was in her dementia. As an only child and without power of attorney nor being a trustee, I was lost and overwhelmed. "Why," I thought, "did they not empower me to be able to help them? Was I not trustworthy?

Was it because I was divorced? Was it because I was a recovering person in the twelve-step program? Why, why, why?"

I know it is not the same as a dear husband, but it was pain and loss and fear to be wandering with my demented Mom and no power to place her in care or handle her finances. This is what led me back to Wisconsin to walk in the Christmas tree fields with my camera, to spot a small tree that looked desperate to grow, and to, in the end, write a best-selling book. *The Littlest Christmas Tree,* now having sold over a million copies, was born in grief.

It was that desperate situation that led me to write the tree story and send it as a Christmas letter to my clients. It was never intended for the public. The last line in the original story said, "Thank you for life, thank you for ideas, and thank you dear _____(*client name here*), for allowing me to speak to your people in this world with its many possibilities."

Out of her own pain and loss Janie was able to write a book that has touched the hearts of many, many people. Perhaps you can do this for someone you love who has experienced their own loss.

Make a Video Movie of Old Family Photographs for the Grieving Person

Justin Spring suggests the following idea:

If you are a close relative or family member who has access to family photographs that might help the grieving person review and remember the loved one who has died, it is possible to scan the photos to turn them into a computer readable format called jpeg that can be used in making a short movie. This can be done on any computer system that has a scanner or at any drugstore that has an automatic photo printing kiosk with a scanner. All Apple computers have i-movie and all IBM computers running Microsoft have Windows Movie Maker that will read the jpegs and put them into a movie format.

Once the photos are read in, you can sequence them and add the loved one's favorite music from a CD and narrate your memories as the pictures pass by. The output can be displayed on the computer or can be downloaded to a digital movie camera that will hook up to your regular TV. Some computer systems have DVD burners that will allow you to output the movie to a DVD.

What a precious gift this would make for anyone who has lost a loved one!

Share the Gift of Music

We all know the saying that "music calms the savage beast." Anyone who is under stress from pain and loss can benefit from the precious gift of music, especially if it is live. If you are a musician yourself, schedule a time to come to play for the grieving person.

Christine Clifford Beckwith shared this idea in her newsletter for the Cancer Club: "Music can truly soothe any soul, so make arrangements to have a musician come to the cancer patient's home for an hour. If the patient has a piano, hire a pianist. If not, a harpist, flutist, or even harmonica player can bring an hour of relaxation and joy to any hurting person. Contact your local colleges, churches, or high schools to see if you can find a volunteer if you do not play yourself. Then make arrangements to join your friend or loved one for your own special concert. It will be an hour you will never forget!"

And her advice to the hurting person: "Sit back, relax, and let the joy of music transpose you to another place and time. Allow your family member or friend to treat you to a special concert created especially for you. Have some hot chocolate, hot cider, or even a bottle of wine on hand to enjoy this special treat. You just might be tempted to take up lessons on an instrument of your own!"

Another way you might use music to comfort is to listen to the loved one's favorite music with your friend or family member.

8. Share Your Own Experiences

You will receive comfort from people who have been in the place of sadness, where you are now. They will be friends, family, and even people you have not known before. In our sorrow, we are all connected.
—Susan Squellati Florence,
When You Lose Someone You Love

To a Compassionate Friend
They told me life never gives you more than you can handle.
Lies, "I can't handle this."
They told me in a year I would be my old self again.
They were wrong. My old self died with my son.
They told me to get my act together and start living again.
All I see is his death.
They said if I were a true believer,
this would be a time of joyous celebration.
"Damn them! I couldn't give him life;
now I can't give him heaven.

You didn't say, "You'll handle this, you're strong."
You said, "Go ahead and cry. I'll wait until you're ready."

You didn't say, "You'll be your old self again."
My old self died too. You helped me find my new self.

You didn't tell me to get my act together.
You said, "Take things slowly, a day at a time.
The pieces will fit when you're ready."

You saw that my faith was shaken; you didn't preach.
You reminded me that He in whom I believe is patient
and understanding.
His love would persevere until I found my way home.

Thank you, Friend, for showing me compassion.
Perhaps I can do for someone what you have done for me.
  —Edith Kmet

Recently I heard a quote from someone that struck a respon-
sive chord in me, "The cracks in your heart are where the light
shines through." When you come to the place in your grief
where you're weary of the hurt, the time may have come for
you to consider using the cracks left in your heart from all the
pain you've experienced to let the light shine through to the
many areas that are still open to you. It can give meaning and
purpose to the life that's left for you and, in the process, your
choice may well help others who have also suffered loss.
  —Mary S. Cleckley

Create a "Pass It On" Gift

Who would ever have thought that a small little brown bear could
have such an impact on so many lives?

In 1999 when my husband, Charlie, was diagnosed with lung
cancer and had to have part of a lung removed, he received a very
special CARE Package from Cheryl Perlitz, a speaker friend of
mine. Accompanying it was this note:

> There are so many who will be with you both all the way through
> this journey, no matter where it leads and how rough and tough it
> gets. Hopefully that will make the path a little smoother for you.
>
> I am sending you this little brown bear that was given to
> me by my childhood friend Marjory the day after my husband,
> Tom, died. Marjory was given this little guy by a friend when
> she was recuperating from colon cancer surgery. When she
> finally knew she was "a survivor," Tom died, and it was time to
> pass him on to me.
>
> Those cute little beady eyes watched over me and reminded
> me that I am loved. For four years I have had him sitting on the

table next to the bed. So now I've finally "rounded the bend," and I think he has another duty to perform. I'll miss him, but I know he will be in the perfect home.

That little brown bear sat on the nightstand next to Charlie's bed, even on the many days when he was in the hospital, until his unexpected death in May 2000. From that day on, I "adopted" the bear as my soulmate and confidant as I worked through the loss of my husband and then a subsequent move two years later that involved the loss of *everything* that was familiar in my life. He bore the brunt of many nights of agonizing tears and aching loneliness, and he was always there waiting when I came back to an otherwise empty home after my many travels and speaking engagements. He truly was an anchor in my life as he had been for Marjory, Cheryl, and Charlie.

Just before Christmas 2004, four-and-a-half years since Charlie died, I began to realize that I was finally nearly whole again. I had made some wonderful friends in my new home, and I truly felt as if I finally "belonged" here. I had started dating and had met some wonderful men, and I had hope and joy in my life again for the first time in the nearly six years since Charlie got sick. I knew it was time to share my little bear with someone else in need.

I had been praying for several days about who needed the bear the most. On Tuesday of that week I received a call from Jeff Fendley, a client of mine who has become a great friend. His dear wife, Caroline, died just months before after an agonizing bone marrow transplant, leaving Jeff with two young sons, Andre, whom they had just adopted from Russia, and Daniel. Jeff has a very stressful full-time job and no family in the area, so he was just holding on by a thread during those days and had no time to even grieve his wife. After that call, I *knew* that Jeff and his boys needed the bear.

That night, amidst a lot of tears, I took several pictures of my angel bear, packaged him up in a pretty gift bag, and the next day mailed him off to my friend, Jeff. A part of me felt as if I were sending away my best friend, and there were a few moments of panic, thinking, "What if something happens and I need him again?" But then my new, stronger self took over, and I realized that this was a life marker moment for me: I no longer needed the constant reassurance that I was loved. I knew that in my heart, and that was enough. And best of all, in my healing, I could share the gift of caring with someone else who really needed a special little friend right now.

Who would ever have thought that a small little brown bear could have such an impact on so many lives? I wonder where his next home might be.

Share Music That Has Been Healing for You or Others

Michelle (Missy) Voller tells her story of a gift of music. After two-and-a-half years of marriage to her wonderful husband, Kirk, she got pregnant, even though her doctor had warned her that conceiving might be difficult.

I was so excited that I could actually conceive! We told Kirk's parents, but I wanted to wait until Christmas to tell mine. I bought a pair of baby booties to wrap up and put under the tree for my parents to open. My mother was in shock and started to hyperventilate. She turned to my dad to show him and tears welled up in his eyes.

The next time we saw the doctor was for our first sonogram. The doctor said he or she was about the size of a green pea so we named our precious baby "Baby Pea." A week or so later, I started to bleed. The doctor asked a few questions and determined that I was okay, but he wanted me to call if it continued. It continued. He decided he wanted to do another sonogram. We saw the baby, larger than the first time. We could see its head and its hands. The doctor said everything looked great and that the baby was about the right size that he or she needed to be at that time. Then, the horrifying news came. The doctor paused and said, "But unfortunately, I don't see a fetal heartbeat." The words hit me like a ton of bricks.

So many things went through my head the next few days. Why me, why us? What caused this? Could I have done anything to prevent it or was it just not meant to be? I think I cried more than I ever had in my life.

Then, one day, an angel of a girlfriend came over. Her name is Caroline, and she helped me get through this time more than she'll ever know. She came with a "Caroline's Catering Service" menu and a bag full of fresh hot food, a card, and a CD. The front of the CD read: "In Memory of Baby Pea" by Watermark—Glory Baby.

She told me that it was a very special song, but that I would have to listen to it when I thought I was ready. Two weeks went by and finally I put the CD in the player. My ears were amazed at how perfect the words were! I cried for hours. I later found out that the singer of Watermark had lost a baby and had written this song for her baby. What a precious gift that song was! It made me realize that I couldn't have done anything differently, and I needed to quit blaming myself. Everything happens for a reason and all in God's timing. Whether the Lord provides children for Kirk and me or not, we'll be okay, just like the singer of the song. We *do* have a baby and someday, we'll see him or her again! Thank you, Caroline!

Be Open; Encourage Others to Share Their Losses

When her mother died, Phyllis Landstrom ordered a large engraved stone that read, "If tears could build a stairway and memories a lane, I'd walk right up to heaven and bring you home again." Then she added a plate on the stone that reads, "Shirley Landstrom, Best Mom Ever." She put it in her garden near her front door, and everyone who visits pauses to read the stone. Then they share stories with Phyllis of their lost loved ones, and she, in turn, gets to tell them about her wonderful mother.

Share Books

Kim Barnhill tells how she and her coworker shared experiences through sharing books:

I have a coworker who recently lost her mother to cancer. She and I are not terribly close, but we had been sharing related stories in the break room about our mothers and our mothers' deaths. I at age eighteen and she at thirty-eight are so very different, and yet our experiences were similar! Two weeks after her mother had passed, I went to the bookstore and purchased *Mothers and Daughters*. I attached her mother's memory card from the funeral inside the front cover, and I wrote a note explaining that life would be forever different for her, but if she would read the book, she would eventually be able to write her own personal story about her amazing mother and the bond they shared.

To my surprise, a week later Pam came by my office to thank me. She explained how difficult things had been and how helpful the book was for her, just to pass the time in the evening. She also mentioned that it was perfect for her coffee table, and it would always have a special place there and in her heart. Later the next week, Pam brought me a book titled *Motherless Daughters*, and she explained that she had bought it to help her cope with the loss but felt like it was geared toward someone who lost their mother at a much younger age, so she, in turn, blessed me with a helpful book. What I learned was that no matter what our age, the grieving process is much the same, and it helps to share it with others.

After Charlie died, my special friend, Rick Jakle, sent me a lovely book titled *A Time to Mourn, A Time to Dance: Help for the Losses in Life.* The note with it said: "You'll note I've written nothing in it, just like the person who gave it to me. That's because it is a 'traveling' book, meant to be passed on to others whose lives we touch who are experiencing loss. This book was meaningful to me and so it is with love and affection that I pass it on to you. When the spirit and opportunity move you, please pass it on to someone else. Know that you are remembered in our prayers."

What a wonderful way to share ongoing messages of hope!

One person shared how books helped her through a difficult time:

My senior year in high school, my grandfather passed away after an unexpected struggle with heart bypass surgery.

My grandfather was the most wonderful man, and I was so blessed to have had him in my life for as long as I did. Despite the fact that he and my grandmother (also a wonderful person) lived in Ohio and my family lived in New Jersey, they never missed a single birthday or holiday with my family. My grandpa was always my entertainer, my game inventor, amusement park riding partner, advice giver . . . oh, I could go on and on. Never have I found someone so deserving of a name as "Grandpa Angel!" He was, and I believe still is, my dear angel.

When I was little, I would always set up a lawn chair in the front yard hours before Grandma and Grandpa were due to arrive. I would anxiously watch each and every car as it would drive by, waiting for the one that would bring my grandparents. I understand that many people feel very fondly about their grandparents, but I want to make clear how dear my grandpa was to me and what a void I felt with his passing.

The night before his funeral, I lay in bed at my grandparents' house, the same house that was now devoid of his hugs, smiles, and calm ways, just crying and crying, questioning why, and going through all the natural responses to losing someone you love.

At his funeral, I don't remember much at all except going through a box of pink tissues at the funeral home. The other memory I have was of a kind and wonderful man from Bowling Green, Ohio, coming up to me and saying that he knew my grandpa and knew why I felt he was such a great person. He asked me a few other questions and said that I would be okay in time.

A few months later, I received a package in the mail. I barely recognized the name on the return address, but inside there were three books and a note. The books in the box were: Og Mandino's *The Greatest Miracle in the World, The Greatest Salesman in the World,* and a book by Leo Buscaglia titled *Love.* The note said that he hoped I had a smile on my face and that he just wanted me to know that he was thinking of me and my grandpa. It was from the man at the funeral home with whom I had spoken.

I don't know if that man will ever know how much that gesture meant to me, but that day, whether or not there was a smile on my face prior to receiving that package, there most certainly was as I read that note. And that smile has not yet faded! I keep those books in my nightstand by my bed. Ten years later when I see those books, I don't particularly remember the words on the pages within. I remember the random act of kindness of the man who cared enough about a girl he didn't even know to make a difference in her life.

I regret that I cannot find the name of that man who touched my life. But if he is still out there, I would want to say thank you from the bottom of my heart for a care package that brings memories of my grandpa close to my heart each time I open my nightstand. Thank you, too, for the reminder that there are people who make a big difference with the little things they do.

Have you ever sent a special book to a person in need, even though you may have just met her or him and even though there is nothing in it for you? That is an angel gift!

Let Others Know What You Have Experienced

Patricia Duffy, who had just shared in the final days of a dear friend, wrote these beautiful, comforting words to me when Charlie died:

> It's chilling to read your odyssey with Charlie after having gone through something similar with my friend who died in January. It's an indescribable journey to walk so close with the breath of death. On one hand there is finality, mortality, suffering, inconvenience, the unknown, chaos. And at the same time exists the sobering reality of what really and really does not matter. Insignificance is so much clearer.
>
> I was told that the last six weeks of a person's life who is suffering from illness is a time to become servant and even slave to that person. And the reason is so that when death has arrived and the soul has departed, we know we gave it our all, our best, and that we are equipped with the fortitude to move forward. A part of grief for many is the "I could have . . . if only I'd . . . I should have . . ." When I totally dedicated myself to my friend her last seven days here, twenty-four hours a day, bathing, feeding, medicating, massaging her, although I was exhausted and in an altered state, when she died, I was able to send her off with great delight. I had given her my very best. So my grieving has been lighter.
>
> I can't change it, and I totally surrendered to it. When I've attended births, I have suspended my work and routines until the baby arrived . . . it was amazing how similar death was. I surrendered my work and routine until the soul left. Both experiences were beautiful and touching and utterly sensational. The loss of my friend left me with a depth that still fills me. My eyes sit farther back in my head now. I look from farther within myself. It's such a teacher, death.
>
> The disruption of "dailyness" is so disturbing at times. Even feeling frustrated at the dying person is hard to accept. And yet it's part of the whole ordeal. All emotions in all situations. You have such a strong support group. I know how invaluable that is and will be. Sadness is a beautiful state of

being. It is hard like a pumice stone, it wears down that part of our smile that is inauthentic. It sinks our spirit into the well of dark ink that drenches our thinking with heavy thoughts that in time become indelible experiences tattooed into the fabric of our soul. Kindness and compassion become our inhalation and exhale. Loneliness and fear become loose threads that tangle our heart, thinner than floss and dissolvable in our memories of how we were able to serve the great soul that was before us.

To know that we help escort a dying loved one to the openness and freedom from restriction of death is so astounding. Someone said death is like taking off a tight shoe or opening a door out of a smoke-filled, noisy room out into the fresh air. What a moment that must be to leave the pressure of this restrictive body and move with grace and mist into the ethers of the blissful infinite!

I send Charlie sweet dreams of freedom and release. I send you strength and grace. They will be yours more than ever when the pain and loss wash away in the bath of hugs and love that shower you every step of your path. It's all so fast and it takes so long. When it's over, it's all new. The toughest part is allowing the fascination of death to be recognized along with the angst. It's an amazing, mysterious thing, the final breath. No one gets out of here alive. I'm so glad we all help each other over the threshold. Charlie is so lucky to have you by his side. What a sense of security. And as was said in *Tuesdays with Morrie:* "Death ends a life not a relationship." Your love for Charlie will be shining brighter than sun on a golden globe. It's permanent. The suffering isn't. Bless your sweet gentle heart.

(When you are grieving) you may want to talk to someone who has traveled his or her grief journey a few miles ahead of you. It really helps to know you are not alone, not "crazy," and not a failure. And if you have misplaced yours for awhile, borrow hope from a friend.
—Sandra L. Graves, *What to Do When a Loved One Dies*

9. Share Good Memories

The mention of my child's name may bring tears to my eyes. But it never fails to bring music to my ears. If you are really my friend, please don't keep me from hearing that beautiful music. It soothes my broken heart and fills my soul with love.
—A grieving parent

What we behold with our eyes is not always what it appears to be. What we can no longer see may be the truly indelible thing, the thing inscribed in the deepest part of ourselves, in the memories we hold in our hearts.
—Nona Martin Stuck, "The Face of Grief"

Memories are ways of recognizing that our loved ones are still a part of our lives. Even though we must learn to live without their daily presence, they will always be in our hearts and a blessed part of our past, so it is important to find ways to share those memories in order to acknowledge that they did, in fact, exist.

Talk about the Person Who Died

When Ana Tampanna's daughter-in-law, who was an officer in the Army, was murdered, Ana requested a service during which her troops could talk about her, offering healing stories for them all. We did the same thing at Charlie's funeral, and what we found was that many of his friends told funny stories, so even in the midst of our grief, we were laughing and remembering the happy times we shared with him.

Nancy Cobb shared that when her mother died, it seemed as if everyone at the wake wanted to tell them a story about her. It helped all of them in their pain to relive her being alive. They showed a video with pictures of her life, so many people there saw themselves with her which triggered many of the stories. Nancy said it was an incredibly uplifting experience for the family and made them all feel so proud to have such a loved person as their mother.

Deb Haggerty said, "When my dad died in 1999, Mom got many notes from folks who'd known him—many of them related a specific incident that they remembered him for—that often made us laugh or cry, but really helped us know that folks cared—about him and about us." When you write notes, the more specific you can be in the memories you relate, the more comforted the family will be.

A man shared with me: "When my mother passed away, I received many cards expressing sympathy. However, the ones that really were special were the ones that included a personal remembrance about my mom. She used to bake the most wonderful homemade bread, and she had a few faithful customers that she would bake for. Several cards brought that memory back to me. Whenever I write a sympathy card, I try to remember to mention my favorite memory of the person that has passed away."

The mother of a child who had died in a freak accident shared: "So many people are afraid to speak to you about your loved one who has died. Many friends and coworkers have never said another word about our son since the day of his memorial service. I wish that others knew it was okay to ask how you are doing and really okay to speak about loved ones who have died. There isn't a day that goes by that we don't think of them. And it is so nice to talk about and hear about my only son that I had for such a short time."

Another grieving parent shares: "We lost our baby at six months, so she was only with us for a day. This is probably very different from someone who lost a loved one they've been with for many years, but at the same time grief is grief. I think some people just don't know how to act and that is understandable. What I have learned is people do need to talk about it. They don't want to forget. In fact, you are going to hurt them more by trying to stay off the subject. My best friend's grandfather passed away, and even though I felt I needed to go to the funeral home, I really didn't feel comfortable. I went straight downstairs to the visiting room to get away from the crowd. While I was there my friend's brother's girlfriend asked me, 'Would you like to talk about your baby? Do you have any pictures?' This made me feel so much better. Just talking about her and keeping her memory alive helps. You will still cry at times, but that's okay. The worst thing is when people say, 'You can have another one.' You cannot replace someone you lost."

Encourage the Person Who Is Grieving to Share Memories

Two weeks after Charlie died, Cheryl Perlitz, a speaker friend of mine who had met Charlie only a time or two, called and said, "I am coming over on Wednesday night, and I'm bringing dinner. I want you to get out your wedding album and all your photo albums, and we're just going to talk about Charlie all night long."

What a precious gift that was to me! It gave me a chance to relive so many dear memories and to talk about the person who was the most important person in my whole life. So many people refrain from talking about a loved one who has died because they don't want to upset the grieving person, but that is just about the worst thing they can do because it negates their very existence. We *need* to talk about our loved ones, and if we cry, that is just fine. Tears can be very healing, and sharing them with a friend creates a bond of the heart that we all desperately desire from one another.

Carol Kramer Leiphart's husband of thirty years died on his way home from work in a car accident. It was the night before their youngest daughters' college graduation and nine months before their oldest daughter's wedding and a week before Christmas. Carol said to me, "Like you, many, many people just let me talk and talk about him and our life together. People really don't know what to say so they just let you talk . . . this is a real gift."

Share Something the Family May Not Know about the Person

Dan Bent of Honolulu shared advice from his mother:

> As a young man when I first experienced having the occasion of expressing condolences to a friend on the loss of a parent, I was at a complete loss for what to say that would be appropriate. I mentioned this to my mother. She gave me what I have found over the years to be excellent advice: "Just say what's in your heart and you'll find it doesn't matter what the words are. The person or family who has suffered a loss will be so wrapped up in the loss

that they won't notice the words you chose, but they will remember and appreciate your intent to be consoling."

I've followed her advice since, and it has helped me overcome the feeling that my words were inadequate. They were, but she was right. The words don't matter, it's the thought that does.

When writing a condolence note to a grieving family I've adopted a simple formula that seems to be particularly appreciated. I express my condolences and then comment on a contact, conversation, or experience with the deceased person that I remember with fondness that is likely to be one that is unknown to the family. That way they get an addition to their own fond memories, and it lets them know that their loved one has had an impact on others.

Create a Video of the Person's Life

A friend shared that when their niece died, they had all the family send them pictures of her as she was growing up, and they created a video collage, added tranquil music, and it was played at the funeral home during the visitation. It also became a keepsake for her family later.

Another person shares what he did for his family members: "This past summer our family lost both my mother at age eighty-seven, and my sister's husband. About five years ago when the small Sony camcorders became the rage, I invested in one. I would attempt to videotape the highlights of every significant event. I have decided to edit these videotapes and create two tapes, one with my mother's activities and the other with my brother-in-law's presence. These edited tapes will be made available for family members who would like a remembrance."

Use the Power of Storytelling

Carol Goldsmith of Washington, D.C., shares how storytelling can heal:

Late on a Monday evening in July, I e-mailed one of the little life lessons (called "carols") that I send to friends and coaching clients around the world. This "Carol on Storytelling" captured some learning I had gained from my dear friend, Bob. As I hit the send button, I thought to myself, "Gee, I haven't heard from Bob in a long time. Maybe he'll read this story and get in touch." Three days later, I received an e-mail from someone I didn't know:

"Carol, we've never met, but I'm Joy, Bob's fiancee. I don't know quite how to tell you this. Bob had a heart attack Tuesday and passed away. As you can imagine, we're all in shock. I just wanted you to know that there will be a service this Friday afternoon."

I couldn't read on through the pool of tears. How could this happen? How did Joy find me? What can I say or do to help now? At the memorial service, I discovered some answers. The last e-mail Bob ever sent to Joy contained an attachment: the "Carol on Storytelling." He did indeed read it, and he got in touch.

The power of story connects us with the spirits of those we have lost, as well as the spirits of those who remain. I've written two "carols" about Bob since his passing. My favorite, "a Carol on Just Desserts," tells how Bob liked to take Joy to a particular restaurant and start the meal with his favorite dessert. Why save the best for last?

This week, Joy and some of Bob's closest friends celebrated what would have been his fortieth birthday in a touching way: by going to his favorite restaurant and having dessert first!

We can celebrate life this very moment. If someone you know is seriously ill, enduring a loved one's illness, or grieving a loss, take a moment now to share a story from happier times. Memories help us stay in touch.

Simple Memories Can Be Powerful!

Darrah Casperson of Glenwood Springs, Colorado, shared what she did for her father: "When mom passed, my father instructed us to remove *everything* in the house that was hers, so we went about the job of doing just that—calling the Salvation Army to take away all her clothes and 'do-dads' that would remind him of her, his most precious thing in life. Now, a year-and-a-half later, he misses all those things, but mostly—her smell. I went to a department store and took one of my mom's old linen hankies and had them saturate it with Chanel No. 5, which was the fragrance she wore, and then I sent it to him. Dad called me when he received the package and was ever so grateful to 'smell' her again. He was afraid to leave the sealed bag open, but I assured him that I could keep that smell coming to him, through her numerous hankies for many years to come. He loved it!"

Each of us has a preferred mode of learning and remembering. For some it is visual, others auditory, kinesthetic, or olfactory. For visually-oriented people, pictures create the best memories. For those who are auditory, tape recordings or videotapes of the person are most powerful. Since we can no longer touch the actual person, a kinesthetic learner will most appreciate the feel of clothing that was special to the deceased person. For a person who is sensitive to smells, the perfumed hanky is something any of us could use, particularly to remember a woman. I always wear "White Shoulders" perfume, so it will be easy for my children and friends to remember me!

Give People Seeds

The family of Shirley Landstrom decided to have a Memorial Service four months after her death because she died in Florida and most of the relatives lived in New York. This gave them time to put together a bound program with color pictures that has become a keepsake item for the extended family. Enclosed in the program were packages of seeds for "Shirley Poppies" . . . so everyone could plant the seeds, and memories of Shirley would continue to grow instead of wither away.

Encourage the Person Who Is Grieving to Keep a Journal

A friend gave me a beautiful journal after Charlie died with this note: "No matter when we lose someone close to us and no matter the reason, it seems there is always something we find we'd like to share. I encourage you to use this journal as you wish to jot down your thoughts to share with Charlie. I know the times since Mom's been gone, I've thought, 'I need to tell Mom this.' The journal gives me a way to share with her still. May it also help you."

Jane Kucera tells about how she was encouraged to journal: "I was fifteen when my mom died. There was very little talk of her after that. Years later, journaling helped me process my mother's death. I was able to put my thoughts on the page, taking them out of my head. I recently talked with a fifty-year-old friend who lost her husband suddenly. She, too, was counseled to journal. She told me how therapeautic it was for her. Another widowed woman I met told me her sister told her to get out and be with other women. She joined my women's writing group and found that helpful. She was not only with us but wrote and shared her pain."

Sandy Donaldson shares another powerful use of a journal to help others: "A dear friend has twin girls and one was in a serious bicycle accident which left her in a coma for approximately three months. She was in college at the time. Her mother did not want her to be alone for one second of the day or night, so she scheduled friends and family to be with her around the clock. We were all scheduled to sit with her in the hospital, but we were not to sit in silence. We were to sing, read books or poetry, play music, pray, and talk to Cary. Then, before we left the hospital room, we were to write to Cary what we did while we were with her. It served as a journal for family members, but happily was a journal for Cary when she eventually came out of the coma. Cary is alive, and I truly believe it was because of the loving support and prayers bestowed upon her. She has the mental ability of an eleven or twelve year old, but remembers some of her past, which I believe is attributed to the stories that were written down and are immortalized for her.

Cheryl Pence of Jacksonville, Florida, shares how her mother, Georganne Eibe, kept a "Fresh Start" journal for her after her husband left her:

On Friday, December 14, my husband of seven years (ten years together) called to tell me he wanted a divorce. (He was away on business for six weeks.) It was completely unexpected. And it devastated me. I immediately called my mom for emotional support. Anyway, she offered to change around her Christmas vacation plans and bought a ticket from Savannah, Georgia, to Sacramento, California, and arrived only four days later.

The following week, Rich and I had a Christmas Cruise planned with my best friend. Of course, he canceled on me, so I took Mom. She and I had a great time. She laughed and had fun with me, and when I needed to cry because I realized I was spending my first Christmas in ten years without Rich, she just hugged me and said that she loved me. After returning from the cruise, we finalized the packing and drove together the more than thirty-five hundred miles to my new home.

My mother was very supportive and remained positive. She kept a journal each day and presented me with a small photo album detailing our journey. By having such a positive spin, "My Fresh Start," the journal became part of the positive new chapter in my life rather than the dreaded closing of the old chapter.

Make a Memory Binder

Sandy Wasik shares how she made a memory binder of her husband with the help of many friends and family:

> Around Christmastime after my husband's death in February, I requested everyone to give me a special present. The gift I wanted was their memories of Matt. I spent hours reading through the treasures that friends and family sent in. The funny thing is that so many of the memories I would never have known. These people knew and saw a completely different side of him than I knew.
>
> When I had gathered all the memories, I added my own and the kids' and put them all in a binder. I made copies for his family and the kids and had them ready just in time for the anniversary of his death. After a memorial Mass, we had a small reception. I had the book there. Since no one who attended the Mass knew Matt, it was a very special way to introduce him.

Live One Day at a Time
Memories—tender, loving, bittersweet.
They can never be taken from you.
Nothing can detract from the joy
And the beauty you and your loved one shared.

Your love for the person and
His or her love for you cannot be altered
By time or circumstance.
The memories are yours to keep.
Yesterday has ended, though you
Store it in the treasurehouse
Of the past.
        —Rabbi Earl A. Grollman, *Living When a Loved One Has Died*

10. Celebrate the Life of the Person

REMEMBER . . . you still have a child.
He is no longer with you.
He is simply in a different place.
But you will always be his mother,
And he will always be your child!
Nothing can change that.

Remember me with a smile and laughter
and when you need me,
Put your arms around anyone
And give to them what you need to give me.
I want to leave you something better than words or sounds.
Look for me in the people I've known or loved
Or helped in some special way.
Let me live in your eyes as well as in your mind.
You can love me most, by letting love live
Within the circle of your arms embracing the frightened ones.
Love doesn't die, people do,
 So when all that's left of me is love . . .
Give me away the best you can.
    —Author unknown

And If I Go
And if I go, while you're still here . . .
Know that I live on, vibrating to a different measure,
Behind a thin veil you cannot see through.

You will not see me, so you must have faith.
I wait for the time when we soar together again.
Both aware of each other.

Until then, live your life to its fullest
And, when you need me,
Just whisper my name in your heart.
I will be there.
 —Emily Dickinson

In the early days of grieving, many of us don't feel much like celebrating, so often these kinds of get-togethers take place later in the grieving process. However, I think we might learn something from other cultures about the way they view loss, especially death. The Balinese have a huge celebration when a loved one dies, and we have all heard stories about an Irish wake. As the friends and family of a grieving person, we have a wonderful opportunity at some time in the grieving process to help them focus on the *gift* of that person or that situation in their lives. By focusing on the positives and the blessings, they are much more able to let go of some of the pain.

Have a Balloon Launch

Ben La Corte of Raleigh, North Carolina, tells of how they used balloons to memorialize his cousin: "My cousin Janice, whom I had grown up with, passed away at an early age from cancer. My Aunt Phil, Janice's mother, was deeply saddened that she was outliving her children. We invited Aunt Phil over for dinner, and many of Janice's family and friends were there. After dinner we assembled in the back yard. Everyone got a marker and a balloon. We told everyone to write a personal message to Janice on their balloons, that we would soon be sending them to her, special delivery. Anyone who wanted to read their special note out loud was encouraged to do so. Then, after some words, we simultaneously released all the balloons. What a dramatic flight! Dozens of glistening tear drops floating heavenward. . . . My Aunt Phil is now with her daughter, but I have no doubt that what we did for her, and ourselves, went zillions of miles toward helping us all cope with our loss, especially Aunt Phil."

Have a "Remember _____ Day" on the Person's Birthday

My son and daughter-in-love, Garrett and Ashley Glanz, began a tradition with our grandchildren, Gavin and Kinsey, to help them remember "Choo Choo Charlie," as Gavin called him. On October 11, his birthday, they always hold a "Choo Choo Charlie Day." They spend time together doing all his favorite things, especially watching sports and playing baseball and golf. (Even though the children are very young, they have fun with plastic bats and golf clubs!) They watch one of his favorite movies, *The Pink Panther* or *A Fish Called Wanda,* and then they have his favorite dinner, either beef stroganoff or "Charlie's chili" and ice cream for dessert. All day long Ashley and Garrett share stories and pictures of Charlie so the children will always feel he is a part of their lives. How grateful I am for their keeping his memory alive!

Celebrate Their Birthday in Heaven

One bereaved mother refers to her son's death date as his "angel date." I love that idea!

Beverly Smallwood, Ph.D., a dear friend of mine, shared a touching story with me. She often keeps her six-year-old granddaughter, Scarlett. On the first anniversary of Bev's mother's death, Scarlett caught Bev wiping a tear. She asked, "What's wrong, BeBe?" Bev told her, "It's been one year since Nannie went to live with Jesus in heaven." Scarlett's eyes widened, "Wow! She's been enjoying heaven one whole year! Can we have a celebration?" Immediately Bev's mood and perspective changed, as she answered, "You bet we can!" The two of them went to the store, got party goods, hats, and favors, and baked and frosted a cake. They invited Scarlett's dad, aunts, and cousins the next day to a delightful celebration of Great Grandma's first birthday in heaven!

Remember Their Birthday on Earth

A woman shares how a friend honored her little son's birthday: "One year after Connor died, one of our dear friends sent us a birthday card on our son's birthday. Inside they wrote about how special he was and how much he meant to them and how they missed him. They made a donation in his name to a children's park, and a stone in a sidewalk there is dedicated in his memory. This was so special to us! I will never forget it."

The Michelini family has found a way to celebrate their loved one's birthday together: "Because my Mom was an only child, she was very close to her cousins and several of them had made it a tradition to drop by on or around her birthday to bring a small gift and have cake and coffee. Mom died in October. The following February was her birthday, and I decided to celebrate it by inviting her cousins and their husbands for dinner. We toasted Mom with a bottle of Asti Spumante (Italian sparkling wine) and celebrated her spirit. Now that I look back on it, that helped not just me, but her cousins too. They were close to her and felt her loss. Sometimes we get so wrapped up in our own grieving that we forget others in the family circle need to mourn the loss as well and why not do it together!"

Mirna Audet shares what her husband did to honor her sister's birthday: "During the first year after my sister's death, my husband brought me an arrangement with four red roses on her birthday. One represented God, one was for me, one for my husband, and one in memory of my sister. I was moved beyond words. It meant more than getting a dozen roses."

A friend shared that her sister's husband, Jerry, died in May 1999. On his birthday in October she still baked two birthday cakes and bought presents for him. The family shared one of the cakes and the other she took to a retirement home along with the gifts. Jerry was always doing things for everybody, so this was a way to keep Jerry's memory alive and give someone else a little joy as well. This idea is one that any of us could do on a deceased loved one's birthday.

One chapter of a support group for parents sends to family members an engraved card on a child's birthday with a note of encouragement. The card is intended to acknowledge this special day and to remember the deceased. Enclosed is a piece of parchment paper on which the child's name is inscribed. It has meant a great deal to those who are the recipients of these cards—someone remembers.

Honor Their Memory by Doing Something for Someone Else

Kate Sorenson tells of what a dear friend did to honor her dad:

"Cheerful Giver" is a perfect description of my dad. He was a giving man, which is evident in all that he did for his family. As a child, I remember the wonderful birthday parties, which have become a special family celebration. Each one of us was made to feel precious, as the family gathered in our honor well past our childhood years until we had families of our own. We've never outgrown the festivities and have passed on the Albright birthday traditions to our own children. Because Dad was such a cheerful giver in every sense of the word, I was touched when my friend honored his memory by assembling and donating a number of birthday bags to children of low-income families. After the flowers wilted and the days got quiet, I knew that Dad would be happy that he made some kids smile on their birthday!

(Note: Cheerful Givers is a national organization that provides birthday bags for needy children. Anyone can participate in this wonderful way of giving. You can find out more information at www.cheerfulgivers.org.)

Drink Champagne in Honor of Their Life

Sporty King, a friend from the Chicago area, tells of how he helped a friend celebrate her mother's life: "A couple of months after a friend lost her mother, I called her up one day before what would have been her mother's eightieth birthday. 'Let's not act like this day will be business as usual. You will be thinking about Mama B. off and on all day tomorrow. So, what time will you finish working so I can come over and we'll drink a bottle of champagne and toast her day and life?' We sat in her backyard among Mama B.'s well-tended garden and laughed about the things she'd said and done to bring joy into the many lives she'd touched. In the process I learned more about my friend, her mother, and their relationship. What I learned has made me a better friend."

Have a "Remembrance" Party

Cyndy Maxey of Chicago shares about a party she had to celebrate her mother's life: "When I lost my mother twenty-three years ago (she was sixty-one) to cancer, I worked part-time at night at a dinner theater as a singing waitress. That group of performers was so outgoing and so supportive! When I invited them to my home to remember Mom (whom they'd all met at one time), they all showed up, and we had a wonderful evening of celebration and remembrance. They each brought a dish or a bottle of wine and talked not only about my mom but others they'd lost and remembered. It was a great release for me and an opportunity to laugh again."

Enjoy Their Favorite "Comfort Foods"

Storeebrooke shares how they have chosen to remember loved ones: "It is said that the sense of smell evokes our memories and so it stands to reason that we seek the comfort of fragrant and palate-pleasing foods to comfort us in remembering loved ones lost. My husband and I traditionally seek out restaurants that we enjoyed with loved ones or that offer their favorite foods. When Grandma Grace passed away, our family went out for spaghetti and lasagna, appropriate because her lineage was Italian! A few years later, we celebrated Grandma Alma's life eating at her favorite Chinese restaurant. Since that time we've indulged in BBQ ribs honoring Uncle Bill, the backyard chef, who followed the trails westward and tantalized the neighbors with the fragrant smoke that floated over his backyard fence at dinner time all summer long!"

Have a Memorial Service That Truly Exemplifies the Person

Storeebrooke's father was unique, so the family designed a unique memorial service for him:

> Daddy Hal was not a conventional dad. He was born on the road, grew up in the circus, played baseball for the army, and made a career of chauffeuring people—both ordinary and famous people, from checkered taxi to airport shuttle to stretch limousine. He liked to gamble, eat spicy food, play jokes, ask riddles, do silly things . . . to laugh and to make others laugh!
>
> Blessed by God's grace and the efforts of loved ones, he had recently opened his heart to accept the Lord. We planned a picnic, invited family and friends, and talked about wearing silly hats and T-shirts. Then my sister said, "Dad's very favorite annual event was your costume party, so let's encourage everyone to come in costume." We knew that our dad wanted everyone to have *fun* at his celebration, and that celebrating life is the appropriate way to say "good-bye." Helium balloons, paper streamers, and family photographs decorated the setting of the memorial picnic. Guests arrived in patriotic T-shirts, safari garb, character

costumes, and one of my brothers even dressed like Dad—plaid Bermuda shorts, a checkered short-sleeved shirt, white striped athletic socks, and brown sandals!

The aroma of BBQ chicken teased us for the feast to come as the chaplain comforted us with God's word. Family and friends listened, smiled, cried, sang, prayed, and shared stories of Dad's childhood circus memories, family celebrations, and accomplishments as well as his vulnerabilities and failures. It was a time of truth, revealing Dad's fatigue, sadness, and disappointment juxtaposed with his courage, happiness, and most of all, peace.

Dad wanted us to remember the good times, to laugh, to love one another, and remember that *life* is meant to be enjoyed. And so, at his memorial picnic, we ate his favorite foods, danced, played games with the children—and said, "So long, see ya later!" to one who enjoyed making us laugh!

Encourage Them to Visit Places the Person Loved

A woman shares how she found peace after her son died:

I had a son who started drugs in high school and was one of those kids who never quite made it into real life. He was clean for up to nine to ten months and then back on drugs. After several years on and off again, he robbed a bank and received thirty years in the Federal Prison system. He then hanged himself after several years of incarceration.

My heart was broken. Selfishly, I would rather see his beautiful face and bright, funny personality in prison than not at all. My brother said he gave me the most important gift he could give me . . . putting an end to visiting different prisons in strange cities, many miles from home. My daughter said, "Mom, think what a life he had. What do you think it must have been like watching your back twenty-four hours a day, seven days a week!"

I was having an awful time, not allowing myself to grieve, staying too busy. A friend offered me a part-time job in Maui, Hawaii, so I retired and moved to Maui. Hawaii had been Jeff's favorite place. He was a surfer and loved the beaches of Hawaii.

Since I was working only a few hours a week, I had the time to walk the same beaches where he had been so happy. He was a young adult with his own life at that time, and I remembered not really listening to him when he talked about his life there.

Now I take the time to look around and see what I think he saw and was trying to share. Now I have the time to visit the restaurant where he worked, the neighborhood where he lived, and even more importantly, I have the time to wander the beach and talk with him. He was there, you see. His ashes were put into the ocean a few miles out from Newport Beach, California. Surely they had reached Hawaii by the time I arrived!

I will always be grateful to the friend who encouraged me and gave me the opportunity to find this peace.

Write a Tribute in the Newspaper
Cheryl Stubbendieck writes about a feature in their newspaper:

Our local newspaper has a weekly feature called "Community Tribute." Readers are invited to write a tribute to someone from the local community who has recently died. I wrote one about our former childcare provider. The lady's husband said he appreciated that his ordinary-but-special wife had been remembered in this way. Publication of the tribute also informed a number of people about the death, since many people routinely read newspapers.

Readers could encourage their local newspapers to initiate such a feature. But even without publication, they can make the effort to put into words the impact the deceased has had. This is different from the first-person thoughts expressed in a well-written sympathy note because it takes a longer view and can use a broader, third-person perspective. Giving such a tribute to bereaved family members would mean a lot to them—especially if given a few weeks after the loss when the grieving family is mourning more quietly and receiving less support.

Writing such a tribute is also a gift to the writer. It forces you to define for yourself exactly the impact the deceased individual had on you—and what your loss is.

Little by little, as we grieve for lost loved ones, we begin to remember not just that they died, but that they *lived*.

11. Keep Remembering the Bereaved Person Even Long after the Loss

As long as we can love each other, and remember the feeling of love we had, we can die without ever really going away. All the love you created is still there. All the memories are still there. You live on in the hearts of everyone you have touched and nurtured while you were here. Death ends a life, not a relationship.

    —Morrie Schwartz, *Tuesdays with Morrie* by Mitch Albon

When you remember me, it means that you have carried something of who I am with you, that I have left some mark of who I am on who you are. It means that you can summon me back to your mind even though countless years and miles stand between us. . . . It means that even after I die, you can still see my face and hear my voice and speak to me in your heart. For as long as you remember me, I am never entirely lost.

    —Frederick Buechner, *Whistling in the Dark*

Old Grief
Older grief is gentler.

It's about sudden tears swept in by a strand of music.
It's about haunting echoes of first pain on anniversaries.
It's about feeling his presence for an instant
One day while dusting his room.
It's about early pictures that invite me
To fold him in my arms again.
It's about memories blown on wisps
Of wood smoke and sea scents.
Older grief is about aching in gentler ways,
Rarer longing, less engulfing fire.

Older grief is about searing pain
Wrought into tenderness.
—Linda Zelenka, Orange Park, Florida

All of us who have experienced a loss of any kind know that grieving is a long-term process. While we are simply trying to get through each day, the rest of the world wants us to "get back to normal" so that they no longer have to deal with the discomfort of our sadness. Therefore, after a few weeks, most people assume that the life of the grieving person is nearly back to normal as their lives are, so they go on about their business and forget that their friend is in terrible pain. I, for example, found that the second and third years after losing my husband and son were even harder than the first!

My friend, Leslie Charles, whose son died, describes it this way: "You and I both know that everyone is there for the first three weeks and then the drop off is staggering. The shock has now worn off, you're trying to get back into a semblance of routine, but the gaping hole in your heart and life has not yet begun to heal, and there are few people to help hold you up. In my book, *All Is Not Lost,* I cite the value of the Chinese tradition of allowing one hundred days of mourning. A note, a phone call (even if you don't know what to say, tell the person you don't know what to say, but you just want them to know you're there, thinking of them) . . . a card—any suggestion of empathy or acknowledgement is deeply appreciated."

My dear friend, Jeff Fendley, shared some thoughts from his experience in losing his wife, Caroline, two years ago and how important it is to keep remembering the grieving person:

Don't assume a person is finished grieving just because they don't express it outwardly. Grief is like having major surgery. It may take a long time to heal and return to normal. Some people take longer than others to heal.

I received a lot of cards, meals, offers of help in the first few weeks. What I remember the most, however, is the help provided six months or more after the event. Even small acts of kindness, a meal, a card, or phone call, said, "I know you are still having a hard time and I'm here for you." This is when I needed support the most.

Here is another thought that is probably common to all who have lost a spouse. I was reminded of this yesterday at church. The question, "How are you doing?" is asked of me most Sundays. As a man, I'm not going to open up and admit my struggles and weaknesses unless I'm sure that someone really cares and wants to listen. I think most men are just being polite when they ask. They suspect my life is hard but don't really want to know. They can't relate to raising children alone and can only imagine how they would cope without their wife. It is something they don't want to think about. The response below is the best way to know if someone is interested in an honest answer:

When people ask me: "How are you doing?" In most cases, I simply respond, "Fine," even if I'm struggling. I don't want to burden people with my difficulties and am not sure they really want to hear an honest response. It is difficult to know if they are just being polite or are genuinely interested. I often don't know how to respond. Do they really want to know how hard my week has been? Do they care that I struggle? Will they consider me a complainer if I tell them how I feel?

I most appreciate those who ask in this way: "I know these last few months have been tough. How are you managing?" This question shows that people understand and don't mind hearing about my struggles. This lets me know I can be open with them. If things are going well, I can certainly correct their impression. But by acknowledging my hardships (any person who has lost a spouse and is now raising children alone finds life difficult), this encourages me to genuinely share how I feel and lets me know this person wants to listen.

Men, more than women, don't know what to say and thus say nothing. It is so hard for them to relate to what I'm experiencing. But women know exactly what it is like to have charge of the children. And so they show concern. I'm praying for an older man at church to become a prayer partner and hold me accountable. It would mean so much to have just one man ask me to lunch to talk about how I'm doing. Single is hard enough, but a single man with young children is really rare, even in the large evangelical church we attend.

Don't be shy to bring up a person's loss for fear of causing them pain. They are already in pain. For many, talking about their loss is a great way to heal. But first, ask if they would mind talking about it. In most cases, they will probably want to talk and appreciate your sensitivity and willingness to listen.

About six months after my husband, Charlie, died, I was invited by a wonderful friend to a surprise birthday party for his wife. Since none of my other friends knew these people, if I went, I would have to go alone. I struggled and struggled with the decision—I wanted to be there for Bonnie, but I *hated* the thought of going all alone, especially when it was an hour's drive away in an unfamiliar place. Because I had been married for nearly thirty-four years, I just never had to do things like this alone, and I was frightened and dreading going without a partner. Finally, at the last minute on the day of the party, I decided I would go just for a short while.

When I arrived, I experienced exactly what I had dreaded—it was all couples except for me! Just as I was about to turn around and leave, Davis Fisher and his wife, Linda, came up to me, gave me hugs, and said, "You are going to sit with us." Then, they proceeded to take me to the table and seat me *in between* them. It was one of the most thoughtful gestures anyone has ever done for me. They were willing to forego sitting next to one another so that I would not stand out as the "odd" one. As a result, I felt perfectly comfortable for the rest of the evening—I belonged somewhere! And best of all, I had conquered one more hurdle in the grieving process, thanks to Davis and Linda. *Please* remember this incident when you are around a widow or widower, and you will bless them in a special way.

A person shares how much it has meant to her to have friends remember her: "In grieving my own *living* losses (a husband with mental illness and a son who has gone to prison), I so appreciate the friends who call me on a regular basis to see how I'm doing, to invite me out for lunch, errands, or a trip to a small tourist area. I appreciate their cards letting me know that they are thinking of me, praying for me. I am grateful for their hugs (which like pancakes are great when warm!). I am grateful for the anonymous gifts of flowers sent on special occasions (Easter, birthdays, Christmas) that remind me that I am not alone, someone is thinking of me."

Remember Holidays and Special Occasions
New Year's Eve
Holidays are always difficult times for someone who has had a loss, particularly the first year. I was especially dreading New Year's

Eve the first year after Charlie died because it was the first time in thirty-four years that I would be all alone, and it also symbolized the beginning of the first year of my adult life without him. I knew if I stayed home alone, I would be horribly sad, but I also dreaded going anywhere to a party where there would be lots of couples. My dear friends, Jack and Pam Burks, recognized this need and invited me to go to South Carolina with them to visit their daughter and her husband over the New Year's holiday. They took me to a lovely mansion for a special dinner and entertainment that evening. Because I was with people I loved in a place that was new, I found a bit of peace and joy instead of the dreaded loneliness I had expected.

A support group for anyone who has lost a child might suggest to a griever that she or he resolve in this New Year to:

1. Take it one day at a time.
2. Let go of any anger that is held inside.
3. Invest in life itself again.
4. Leave behind the bad times and take hold of the good times.
5. Value what's left of life.

Add to this list ideas of your own that are unique to the one who is in grief.

Valentine's Day

Pam and Jack Burks blessed me again on my first Valentine's Day without Charlie. On February 14, 2001, they sent me a beautiful flower arrangement with a note telling me that even though I would not be getting a valentine from Charlie, they wanted me to know that I was still loved. Remember your grieving friends on this "Holiday of Love." When others are sharing their joy, they are feeling horribly alone.

A friend tells of how she helped another friend celebrate Valentine's Day:

> This past Valentine's Day, I ministered to a friend whose partner had committed suicide. I invited her out to lunch (booking the private dining room in my favorite restaurant) and treated her to good food and fellowship and I listened as she shared her

heartache with me. It is important when grieving any type of loss to know that there are people who care enough to listen.

I had felt inspired to purchase several pins from Avon with a little angel hovering over a very bright red heart. I gave my friend one of these and told her that I believed God had assigned an angel to her broken heart, and she was not walking this path alone. She opened the tiny box and started to cry, "This is so precious." The words came from deep within when I responded, "Your heavenly Father wants you to know that you are precious to him now and as you journey through this dark valley of grief." It was a powerful lunch, and I was able to affirm to her the strengths I saw in her and to affirm the sacred moments she shared with her spouse.

Halloween and Thanksgiving

The last three months of the year can be very difficult for everyone, especially the grieving person. Offer to purchase Halloween candy and bring over a pumpkin or two to set on the front porch. If they have lost a child, something that would mean a lot would be for you to answer the door and give out the candy, so they would not have to see the other children and remember even more poignantly their own loss.

At Thanksgiving, bake a turkey with all the trimmings and take it to the hurting family. In some ways this can be the hardest holiday of all for a grieving person because it is very difficult for them to be thankful. All they can see, for several years sometimes, is what is missing in their lives.

You could make them a Thanksgiving tree like we have in our family so that they could begin again to find some blessings in their lives. Many years ago I took a large manzanita branch, sprayed it gold, and secured it in a base of plaster of Paris. Beside it I kept a basket of small plain cards with holes punched in them, another basket of pieces of colored yarn, and pens. The tradition in our family is that the month before Thanksgiving, the tree is placed on a table in our living room, and all month long each family member writes down things for which he or she is thankful and hangs them on the tree. We also encourage guests in our home to participate—even our mail carrier likes to come in and write his thank you's. At the dinner table on Thanksgiving Day we read the cards from the tree as an affirmation of our blessings. Then we save the cards from the year before, and we read those as well. It is a wonderful way to remind us of all the goodness in our lives.

Christmas

Here are some suggested ways to help others through the holidays:

- Give a gift in memory of the loved one.
- Hold a special memorial service for them at the holiday time.
- Make a special ornament for their Christmas tree in memory of the loved one.
- Share responsibilities for meals, decorating, or wrapping gifts.
- Offer to shop for them.

For the grieving person, the anticipation of any holiday can be much worse than the actual holiday itself, so we need to be there for them in the weeks ahead, helping them prepare.

A dear friend shared with me that they had always made a big deal of Christmas, so after her husband died, she gave a friend her credit card and asked her to buy some presents from him. She said, "I needed so badly to have some surprises."

Create a "Christmas Cheer Box" for someone. Maybe you are wondering how you can help someone get through the holidays in the midst of severe problems, illness, or grief. Here is the story of how one idea helped and how it continues to multiply every year:

Carlene Eneroth of Spokane, Washington, lost her husband from a massive heart attack when he was only thirty-one years old. Even though her whole world had come to a screeching halt, Carlene was flabbergasted to discover that life was moving right on, even though her grief had kept her out of touch. Most of all, she dreaded her first Christmas without Greg.

On Thanksgiving weekend her parents arrived with a big, open-topped box, covered with bright Christmas wrap and containing many small, gaily-wrapped presents inside. Carlene said, "At first I wanted to scream, cry, run, and hide. Didn't they know I didn't want anything in my home that spoke of this awful upcoming holiday season?"

Her mother put the box on the table and explained that since all of them couldn't be together for Christmas, she wanted this box to help her through the hard month ahead. She suggested Carlene unwrap one present each day. Carlene thanked them and then quickly shoved the box over in the corner behind a chair, hoping to forget its very existence.

After a bad day at work on December 1, Carlene remembered those presents and decided to open one. She found a classy new pot holder. The next day she woke up to a "gray" day when, for no reason except her grief, everything was awful. She opened another present—some cute little note pads. Each day she amazed herself by giving herself "permission" to open another little present (knee-high stockings, new ball point pens, garden gloves, envelopes of hot chocolate, stationery). Each one subtly reminded her that Christmas was coming whether she liked it or not, and she might as well face it. But most important of all, for a few minutes every single day, she felt loved and remembered.

A couple of years later when she met a young woman and her three little children who had recently lost their dad to suicide, she remembered her mom's box idea. She said: "I wasn't sure how I could create a 'Cheer Box' for a whole family, but I wanted to try." After her first experience, Carlene was encouraged to continue, and now she does one or two boxes a year. She begins buying little items she sees on sale all through the year and, when November comes, she is ready to begin planning on who needs a box and what to put in it. One church group decided their Ladies' Circle would try the idea. Each person brought three days' worth of presents.

After the death of Carlene's family doctor last summer, his medical office adopted this idea as something to be done for his wife. A parent on one of the soccer teams in her area suddenly died, and the team parents got together with this idea and made up a fun box for the entire family.

©Barbara Glanz 1998. Reprinted with permission from *Care Packages for the Home*.

A "Holiday Cheer Box" would be a marvelous family project whether your family is made up of one or two persons or several. Think about someone who is having a struggle near the holiday season and then put your care into constructive action. As Carlene says, "The ideas and possibilities are endless!"

Help with a Christmas tree. Our second little boy, Gavin Ward Glanz, was born on December 21, died on December 22, and was buried on Christmas Eve, which is the day many of us celebrate the *birth* of a baby. After that devastating experience, It took me nearly five years to really enjoy Christmas again. When Charlie died, I truly dreaded that first Christmas, especially since only one of my children could be home.

In the past, like most mothers, I had spent days baking, decorating, and shopping, yet this year I just had no energy to do much of anything. As a result, I decided not to have a Christmas tree since I would be leaving for South Carolina soon after and I had *never* had to shop for a tree alone. I wasn't even sure if I could really manage it, let alone the emotion of having to do it for the first time. (We had always had a real tree, and it was part of a special tradition we had of picking out the tree on Thanksgiving weekend and then going to a favorite place for lunch.)

Two days before Christmas, a new friend, Nancy Cobb, called and said she was coming over with her SUV, and together we were going to get me a Christmas tree. I will never forget the feelings of gratitude I had! Even though we had to settle for a "Charlie Brown" tree since they were all picked over, it was the nicest tree I have ever had because it came from such thoughtfulness and love.

Cheryl Perlitz tells about how someone whose name she didn't even know made her Christmas special:

> I was married twenty-nine years. Every single year, without exception, we went through the same routine buying a Christmas tree. I would get the house clean and ready to receive the tree. I would stage the Christmas music, ready for action in the CD player next to the fireplace. Every year I went to the grocery store and bought bags full of hors d'oeuvres and bottles of spiced apple cider to fix as soon as we got back with the tree.
>
> The year after Tom died, only my youngest boy came home from college for a lonely Christmas with just me. I was determined to make it a traditional Christmas for him in at least in a few small ways. The day before he was to return home, I made my regular trek to the grocery store for the hors d'oeuvres and

cider. I put them neatly in the kitchen and then carefully placed the Christmas CDs next to the fireplace and CD player.

Off I went with my checkbook, Christmas tapes for the car, and my ball of twine to tie the tree onto the car. I drove to my old high school Boys Club tree lot. I parked the car and put my hand on the cold door handle. I couldn't move. I was simply frozen . . . and then the tears started falling. I just couldn't do it. It wasn't the same. My husband was gone and so was the tradition and all of those warm, comfortable Christmas tree feelings.

So I decided to breathe deeply and set off for another tree lot. Maybe it would be better to go to a place that was in a different part of town. I drove two suburbs over to a place where I had never been. I blasted that Christmas music in the car as high as it would go and finally pulled into a parking spot right in front. This time I got the car door part of the way open, put one foot on the ground and . . . the tears started to fall again. I just couldn't do it.

"Okay," I said to myself. "You have to go into this lot and get the tree." But I just couldn't make myself do it, so I decided to "take care of myself" and put it off for another day.

Instead, I decided to drive to the town I had moved from about four months before, just after my husband died. My friend had stored my Christmas decorations at her house there and at least I could pick them up and get something done. I also knew those boxes were waiting for me outside of her house, so I wouldn't have to face anyone with puffy red eyes. The one hour drive to Barrington was silent.

The boxes were sitting there waiting for me. Mission accomplished! "Okay, the tree can wait until tomorrow."

As I silently left and started to drive home, I happened to notice the old Christmas tree farm lot where Tom and I had bought our trees for many years. I took a deep breath and drove in the driveway. I was the only car there, but just as I drove up, a farmer, smiling broadly, came out of the little farm house.

"Oh, hi!" he said. "We were hoping you would come. I have a tree here in the corner waiting for you. We heard you moved away, but we were just hoping you would come to get a tree. Your husband really lit up our lives every year with his big smile. We were so sad to hear that he had passed away, and we just want to give you this perfect tree to show you that we care."

I just stood there feeling such gratitude. He cut the bottom off the tree straight and flat, wrapped it in a plastic sheath, and instructed me on how to get it up the elevator and in the stand. And I didn't even know his name.

Help people change holiday traditions

A bereaved parent shared that since her son's death, at Christmas she buys everyone in the family an ornament that reminds her of him. Then friends and family give her Christmas ornaments to hang on their new "Andrew" tree. It helps her know that Andrew has not been forgotten.

One mother shared how important it is to change holiday traditions after a loved one dies or even after a divorce or breakup. Instead of decorating in the same way she had in the past, she tells what she did differently to help take some of the pain away:

> I found a tiny artificial tree which I placed in my daughter's room this year and decorated it with the silly earrings we had collected over time. In her memory, I pick a pair of earrings off the tree each day to wear and put them back in the evening as I go about plugging in the window candles. Last year I got her a purple stuffed bear which is once again sitting on the mantel with her picture above her hanging stocking.

She even suggested a way to change things in their gift giving at the office. Be an encourager to help your friends and family members who have suffered a loss to find new traditions to help ease the pain. Be there to *help* them with tasks that are overwhelming, like the shopping, decorating, and baking, and suggest some new things that can add a tiny measure of new joy to their holiday.

Another person shared how hard the holidays were for her because she could not buy her son a gift ever again. However, her Bereaved Parents/USA support group decided to start a new tradition. At their December potluck, they are each asked to bring a gift that is something they would have bought for their child if he or she were alive. The gifts are then taken to a local children's home. She says, "On Christmas morning when my surviving children are opening their gifts. I sit back and picture a child that probably would not have gotten a gift at Christmas, opening the gift that I bought for Matthew. That gives me such peace." This is a tradition you may want to start in your organization if you have bereaved parents as members.

Loved one's birthday and death day

A friend wrote, "I wish that on the anniversary of my child's death extended family members would remember her. I also wish that they would remember the day she was born because although she is no longer here, she is still loved and missed, and it still hurts."

Think about your friends who have had losses. Do you remember to support them on these special dates? I have one friend who always sends me a card on the anniversary of my husband's death. It means a great deal to me that someone in this wide world remembers!

A person shared how they celebrate their daughter's birthday: "We choose to celebrate her birthday in October. We gather friends and family together, perhaps lunch out, or if nice weather, perhaps a picnic. We spend the time in happy conversation, speaking of our girl with love and fond memories. After we are all full from our meal, we take a trip over to the grave where we hang little personal messages onto balloons and then let them loose. It has proven to be a very moving, but happy time. It's always good to know that people remember!"

Mother's Day and Father's Day

One woman I spoke with said that she wished on Mother's day people would remember her, because even though her only child died, she is still and will forever be, a mother.

Kathy Pacey and her husband lost their only child, Tommy. She writes this about Mother's Day: "I want to share what my precious neighbor, Meg, has done for me each and every Mother's Day. Tommy is our only child. Since he died, my family didn't know how to handle that day, but, thankfully, my friend Meg did. Every year she takes the time to plant blooming flowers in the whiskey barrel on my front stoop with her daughter, Maggie, who happened to be Tommy's best friend (yes, at three years old he had a best friend already!). Maggie keeps in touch with me, always remembering his birthday and death day. I feel so blessed to have her in our life."

Hospice of Lancaster County, Pennsylvania, has sponsored a memorial Mother's Day Brunch, "Remembering Our Mothers—A Gathering of Women Whose Mothers Have Died," to provide an opportunity for women to remember the most important persons in their lives. Patti Homan, manager of the Hospice PATHways Center for Grief and Loss said, "There aren't enough opportunities to remember. We live in a quick-fix society." What a special way for women who share a common loss to be blessed with the chance to remember their departed mothers!

Remember fathers who have lost a loved one, especially on Father's Day. Some men find it difficult to express their feelings and yet need to know that you are there to support them in whatever ways seem appropriate. One man writes about the kindness of a neighbor:

> Today is Father's Day. It's not a day I treasure or celebrate. As I was standing in the driveway washing my car, a neighbor came out of his house and walked over to me.
>
> "I was thinking about you all day today. How are you feeling?" his question truly surprised me.
>
> I stammered the usual, "I'm okay, thanks for asking!" never intending to tell him that he just brought me back to reality from a quiet time mourning my daughter.
>
> He told me that he didn't know her very well, and would I consider telling him all about her . . . Wow! Nobody ever makes that request from me!
>
> I talked for quite a while about what a great kid she was, her dreams, her accomplishments, where I thought she would be today had she not died.
>
> He just listened to all I had to say, smiled and told me that he wished he had gotten to know her better. He told me that she was obviously someone very special, as he noticed the sadness in my eyes ease as I talked about the good things. Then he shook my hand and told me how lucky I was to have had such a great girl.
>
> He went home, leaving me in wonder of how he pulled me out of a slump I had been in most of the day.

Life marker times

Penny Wallace of Battle Creek, Michigan, writes about how her son's classmates thought of her many years after his death:

I have an angel who is always looking over me—my son, David. On May 25, 1989, David was killed in a head-on collision caused by a reckless driver. David was eight years old.

David was in the second grade with only three weeks to go before the summer vacation was to begin. He was a very active eight year old, involved in ice hockey, soccer, and baseball. He was especially looking forward to his first year in rocket football.

His death was devastating to the entire community. We received an overwhelming response and support from his class-mates, teachers, fellow teammates, coaches, and friends.

The parents of his classmates collected money and pur-chased benches for the playground at the school in memory of David. The Ice Hockey Association, David's teammates, and parents, had a dedication ceremony on his tenth birthday. A flag pole and bronze marker was permanently laid outside the hockey rink in memory of David.

On June 1, 1999, David was supposed to graduate from high school. Another milestone missed, another hurdle to overcome. As graduation neared, those around me were planning celebrations for their graduates, and graduation announcements were being sent. What would have been David's senior year was coming to an end; the air was filled with excitement. As I tried to share in the excitement of those around me, inside my heart was breaking. One of the most exciting times for a child and his or her parents was one of the most miserable for me—I had nothing to celebrate.

Then my earth-bound angels appeared—a day never to for-get. It was a Sunday, May 15, only sixteen days until graduation. I had just returned home when several cars pulled into the drive-way behind me. I turned to see what all the commotion was and there before me stood my son's classmates. As they approached me, they tearfully presented me with a beautiful bouquet of flowers and a 1999 Yearbook—dedicated to my son. There in the pages of the senior class portraits was an enlarged picture of my son, David. Beside it was a special poem written by his girlfriend from the second grade. Each page was signed by his classmates with poems, stories, and good-byes.

His classmates gave us special passes to attend the bac-calaureate and graduation ceremonies. On graduation night David's best friend tearfully gave me a graduation tassel to keep to honor David. A unique senior tradition in our community is making a video which includes snapshots of special events, special times, and special friends during the school years of that class. The video is shown during the baccalaureate ceremony. To my surprise, the video included pictures of David with his classmates in their younger years, together with a special dedication in his memory.

Words cannot express the heartfelt joy and pride these individuals have brought to me. His classmates demonstrated how special he was to them by celebrating and commemorating his eight short years of life and the impact that life had on them.

They made a very difficult, almost unbearable, time for me very special. They made me feel very much a part of this milestone in their lives, as well as in what would have been a milestone for David. Thanks to my earth-bound angels for making the impossible . . . possible.

Invite Them Out

This is an obvious thing to do, and yet so few really do it beyond a few weeks after the loved one has died. The rest of the world goes on as if nothing has happened, while the grieving person's life has nearly stopped. Each day is a struggle, and the thought of going out somewhere is overwhelming, often for months and months.

When you call to ask the person, be encouraging and firm. Tell them that you will pick them up at such and such a time and what the dress is. Be sensitive to where you are going to take them. If a spouse has died, it is best not to go to a romantic restaurant where there will be many couples. If a child has died, *never* take them to a park or a family restaurant during a time when there will be many children around.

Remember them especially on the weekends as these are the hardest days of all for grieving people. Others are spending time with their families, and they are all alone. A friend recently shared with me that Sundays still are hard for her, even though her husband died a number of years ago, since that was the day that they always blocked off to spend together. Invite hurting people to do things on Saturday or Sunday when at all possible.

Linnea Berg shared how much it meant to her when people included her father after her mother died: "Several members of mother's high school reunion committee asked my father (who grew up on the East Coast, nowhere near Riverside, Illinois) to continue to attend their reunions and planning meetings. Whether he does or not, it made him feel as if he belonged to the gang just as much as she did."

This is what one woman wrote that she wished people had done when her father died: "I wish my mother's friends would have taken her out for dinner and not just assumed she was okay. She was so lonely, and it was as if no one but me noticed and I was so sad, too—I wasn't much good in the cheering up department!"

Keep Sending Cards and Notes

So often we send cards and notes right after a loss and then we get busy and go on with our lives. One of the most thoughtful things we can do is to remember people in the long months after the initial loss. A precious speaker friend in Illinois made it a point to call me once a week for months after my husband, Charlie, died, just to make sure I was all right. I will never forget how much those calls meant to me.

Kathy (Morrison) Ditlevson tells about another person who cared: "Another gesture that meant so much to me was that a man in my church continued to send me cards of encouragement, even six or seven months after my husband died. Those cards seemed to come at just the right time when I needed some words of hope and knowing that someone was still thinking about me and praying for me."

A friend shared, "When someone is grieving or has experienced a loss, instead of or in addition to sending a sympathy card, I send an uplifting or inspirational card. I will usually buy more than one and send the cards out over the following weeks to come. This has never failed. I usually get a hug and a special thank you every time."

Give Them a "Wednesday Blessing"

Ruth Gagnon tells about what her friend, Linda, did to help her get through the first year in Toronto, Canada: "Within days of my husband, Peter, being killed, my friend, Linda, made a commitment to give me a 'Wednesday Blessing' for a year. Every Wednesday after work she would come over with her two children and bring me a special coffee and spend time with me. Sometimes her husband would join us and it would spontaneously turn into supper!

It made all of us stop what we were doing and be together. We have all become close friends and love this family dearly. Her gift of a regular time to look forward to gave us all a lifeline."

Offer to Take Their Children for a Weekend

If the person who has had a loss is now a single parent, especially if they have no family near, they may have no chance to simply "get away" alone and have some time for peace and meditation and healing. Jeff Fendley, who is now the single parent of two young boys since his wife died, shared with me that the best gift anyone could give him while he is working through his grief would be to take his boys for a weekend so that he could have some time to himself. He works full-time and then comes home to make dinner, clean, do the laundry, help with homework, and then get the children in bed. He has no time just for himself to pray and think and heal.

12. Do Little Things That Add Joy to Someone's Day

Owe nothing to anyone, except to love one another; for the one who loves another has fulfilled the law.
—Romans 13:8 (NAB)

Be kind and merciful. Let no one ever come to you without coming away better and happier.
—Mother Teresa

Beginning today, treat everyone you meet, loved one or stranger, friend or foe, as if they were going to be dead at midnight. Extend to each person you meet, no matter how trivial the contact, all the care and the kindness and the understanding and the love that you can muster. And do so with no thought of any reward. Your life will never be the same again.
—Og Mandino, *A Better Way to Live*

When a person is grieving, the tiniest thoughtful thing can turn their whole day around. Soon after my husband died, I began keeping a "Blessings Journal." At the end of each day I would force myself to think about what had happened that day that was a blessing to me. Most of the time these would be very small things—a call, a card, an invitation, a smile of encouragement, a small gift, something I read. What was most amazing to me, however, was that even on the darkest days, I could always find a blessing or two if I really tried—and nearly all of them came from people reaching out to me.

Create an "Everyday Survival Kit"
Months after Charlie died, a friend sent me a darling little bag filled with the following things and the card with it read as follows:

Toothpick: To remind you to pick out the good qualities in others.

Rubber band: To remind you to be flexible. Things might not always go the way you want, but it will work out.

Match: To remind you to light your fire when you feel burnt out.

Band aid: To remind you to heal hurt feelings, yours or someone else's.

Candle: To remind you that you can brighten someone else's day.

Pencil: To remind you to list your blessings every day.

Eraser: To remind you that everyone makes mistakes and it's okay.

Chewing gum: To remind you to stick with it and you can accomplish anything.

Mint: To remind you that you are worth a mint to your family and friends.

Candy kiss: To remind you that you are loved.

Tootsie Roll: To remind you not to bite off more than you can chew.

Smarties: To remind you on those days you don't feel so smart.

Starburst: To remind you to get a burst of energy on those days you don't have any.

Snickers: To remind you to take time to laugh.

Tea bag: To remind you to relax daily and go over that list of your blessings.

To the world you may just be somebody—but to somebody, you may be the world (like me)!

This made me smile, and it made me feel as if someone really did care about me, long after most of the world had forgotten my loss.

Think of Little, Thoughtful Surprises

My husband, Charlie, died in May, and in July I was scheduled to attend a convention of the National Speakers Association for several days. This would be the first time I had seen many of my speaker friends, who live all over the world, since his death.

When I arrived to check in, the person at reception told me that there was a package waiting for me. Upon opening the package, I found that a friend of mine had given me several pocket-sized packages of designer tissues, some with little flowers, some with butterflies, and some with tiny animals. She knew that this would be a difficult and emotional time for me, so she wanted to be sure that I was prepared! I will never forget this precious, thoughtful little gift.

Soon after her son died and her husband left, a woman tells this story of love: "I was working in a church office and it was a cloudy, bitter day in January. I had been driving on bald tires. Later in the day I got a call from Circle O Tire Company in Lynnwood. 'We are ready to put the tires on your car,' they said. 'But I didn't order tires,' I replied. 'Who ordered them?' 'We were told *not* to tell,' was their response. I could never find out who it was until a friend, Del Miller, died of a brain tumor, and I was asked to sing at his service. As I prepared to sing, his daughters told me that it was he who saw my bald tires and ordered new ones. Del was known for these many random acts of kindness."

Make a "Grieving Gift Basket"

Alyice Edrich shared her idea of a "Grieving Gift Basket." It would include a grief journal, pen (lost one's favorite color), candle (favorite smell of lost one), prayer book (one that consoles the soul), blanket or clothing that belonged to the lost one, soothing musical tape, and a box of tissues.

Take Care When Sending Cards

Mirna Audet, who lost one of her sisters, shares some cautions when sending cards:

1) Always send a sympathy card or a thinking of you card. Try to avoid writing, "She's in a better place." It doesn't help those in pain. A good choice of words is, "We love and miss her too." If you didn't know the one who passed away personally, another choice would be, "I'm thinking of you in a very special way."

2) After sending a sympathy card, it's always a good idea to send a "thinking of you" card whenever possible. I've heard from many people that they love getting cards and that they do help. It lets them know you care.

3) Be careful during the holidays when sending greeting cards. When someone is still grieving, the last thing they want to see is Santa with a big smile on his face. I like sending nature scenes that

are serene. People want their pain acknowledged and respected. It's part of the grieving process.

A woman shares a delightfully creative idea for sending cards: "I had breast cancer nearly thirteen years ago, and while I was going through a difficult chemotherapy, an acquaintance who taught in the same department I did sent me a number of 'thinking of you' postcards from his cats. Each one was just a plain blank postcard with a hand-written sentence wishing me a good day, warm thoughts, or something else equally ordinary. But each card was 'signed' by his eight cats, and marked with random paths of paw prints across the card. Of all the get-well cards I received, of all the things people did for me during that time, I remember best those funny little postcards and the smiles they brought to me."

Another person shared that she purchases fifty-two cards when someone has had a loss and then sends them a card a week for the whole first year. Some are serious and some are funny, but each one says to the suffering person, "I am thinking of you." In the envelopes she often includes coupons for places like coffee shops, movie theaters, and bakeries with a note that says, "When you feel better, we are going to go here."

Surprise People with Small Gifts

Mirna Audet also shares, "It's a great idea to give a gift to the one who lost a loved one. I went to a bath-products store and put together a few of their beauty products for someone I barely knew. When her husband gave the gift to her, he said that she started to cry. She couldn't believe that someone cared that much about her."

Karen Yoho of Alexandria, Virginia, shares this idea: "I think one of the hardest roles there is to play in life is to be the comforter of someone who has lost a loved one. You feel so very helpless. A few times I have been called upon to play that role and remember something I read by Leo Buscaglia about making a big chocolate cake and delivering a bunch of wild flowers. . . . Tell them there are still wonderful things in the world to eat and beautiful things to see . . . that they must not give up and to live on to experience all that life has in store for them."

I recently received this thank-you note from June Wilson, a lovely woman who was in my church and who read about this book project: "We read of your book project and remembered how you ministered to us in the past. I had been in and out of the hospital a number of times without any immediate solution to my problem. On one occasion, I opened our front door to see your sweet smiling face. You came personally to deliver a tape (Joyce Landorf's "Balcony People"). You also brought a colorful child's craft made by one of your sweet daughters. I still have it—the Eye of God. It is a reminder that God is ever present. I played the tape again and again and found an inner strength and peace in the midst of my struggle. I just wanted to encourage you in this aspect of your ministry. God has gifted you with a compassion and abilities to minister to hurting people. I believe he will honor your efforts with this new book."

It had been many years since I had made that visit, so we never know the impact a small kindness can make on someone.

Give the Person a "Prayer Beeper"

Sandy Donaldson was the "Samaritan" in this story that appeared in the newspaper:

> The woman who was the point person on a creative campaign to help a sick friend says that who commits a caring act isn't as important as its potential use by others for someone special in their lives. So, in the interest of sharing, we are honoring the requests for privacy by referring to them as the Samaritan and the friend. When the friend was going to have a mastectomy at a North Carolina hospital, the Samaritan followed an idea that came to her via a newspaper clipping someone had passed along. "I purchased a beeper," the Samaritan says. "I made a list of people who I knew would like to pray when my friend had her surgery at Duke. I gave those people the beeper number, and each time they prayed, or thought of her, they were to call the number and input their phone number."
>
> The friend was given a list of people who would be praying for her. When someone called, she could look down the list and see who was thinking of her at that very moment. "She was not allowed to call anyone back," says the Samaritan, "That was the deal—as that would have been too overwhelming for her to accomplish." The Samaritan put the numbers in a frame so her friend could keep them by her bedside. "After having it for a few

days, just the support it gave me was immeasurable," the friend says. "People come up with the most creative ideas. It's nice to know what different things you can do."

The Samaritan and other caring people also organized meals for when the friend had post-op treatments, both in and out of town. Some of the meals she carried with her to North Carolina. Others, the Samaritan brought to the house, letting herself in with a key while her friend rested. More gifts from the heart? The weekly flower arrangement sent to the friend during her course of radiation in North Carolina.

Sandy said, "I want to share this idea with you as I think it is a wonderful idea for the person who is ill as well as the persons praying for the person who is ill—a win/win for all!"

Create a Video "Letter"

The National Speakers Association chapter has done something very special for one of their members which Patt Schwab shared: "Steve Holtzer, past NSA Northwest president, recently had pancreatic cancer. Because there was little communication from his family, we were unsure how his health was or how high (or low) his hopes were. Many of his friends in the chapter wanted to do something beyond the get-well card level that was not overly intrusive. The result: About twenty of us made a video "Christmas letter" for him with a variety of one-to-three-minute clips. The goal was a series of upbeat, funny news bits catching him up on our lives and letting him know he was in our thoughts. The clips were made individually or in small groups. Not only did we hope it would touch his heart, but it has also been a community builder for those of us involved in sharing his pain."

Make a Golden Prayer Bowl

When Robert Henry, a much-loved member of the National Speakers Association, was ill with cancer, Ginger Plowman sent a request to all of us to help put together a prayer bowl for Robert:

Because Robert has touched the lives of so many, I am appealing to you to join me in giving something back to him, something that will encourage, bless, comfort, and inspire him during this trial—some season of his life, something that is powerful enough to make an eternal difference.

Revelation 8:3-4 says, "Another angel, who had a golden censer [bowl], came and stood at the altar. He was given much incense to offer, with the prayers of all the saints, on the golden altar before the throne. The smoke of the incense, together with the prayers of the saints, went up before God from the angel's hand."

Wouldn't it be neat to present Robert with a golden bowl full of prayers? There is no greater gift, no greater comfort, no greater blessing, and nothing more powerful that you could ever offer him than the power of your prayers. Perhaps one day, those of us who have trusted Jesus, will receive a golden bowl of the prayers that were offered up on our behalf. What a treasure on earth this gesture of love and faith will be to Robert and his family! In response to this request, please e-mail me a prayer for Robert or send a message letting him know that you are praying for him.

Give Pampering Gifts to Encourage Someone

When someone is grieving, they have no thought of themselves; they are simply in survival mode, so doing something that brings them joy and focuses simply on them is a precious gift. Present them with a gift certificate for a massage, facial, manicure, or pedicure to help soothe their soul and brighten their spirits. Even a simple certificate for a shampoo and blow dry can mean the world to someone who is simply trying to get through each day. Then, offer to make the appointment, pick them up, and drive them home. You will be giving them a gift of relaxation and joy.

For a man, you may want to give them a certificate to play a round of golf, hit golf balls, or go to a gym. Again, be there to arrange it and drive them. Let them decide if they want to be alone or to have your company.

A friend shared that when her father died, her best friend was not able to be there for the funeral. So, instead, she sent her a beautiful fluffy pink robe and scuffs with a note that said, "Every time you put this on, feel my arms around you, letting you know *you are loved!*" What a precious way to share her love in an ongoing way. My friend says that each time she puts on that robe, she feels comforted and loved.

Have a "Bring Back the Joy" Party

When her husband's parents and her mother died and things were pretty tough for them, Colleen Nordlund decided to have a "Bring Back the Joy" party for their friends and family. She asked each of them to bring their favorite fun food. They brought ice cream, popcorn, red licorice, and one person even brought a sand pail filled with pudding and crushed Oreos so it looked like dirt! After all the guests arrived, she gave everyone pens and paper and asked them to write down the "joy busters" in their lives. Then they went outside, put all the papers in a barrel, and burned them! Later they played fun games like Cranium, Twister, and Pictionary. When everyone got ready to leave, Colleen gave them all gift bags filled with the following: Almond Joy, Snickers, Jolly Ranchers, Smiley face erasers and notepads, Bible verses about joy, and confetti. She said everyone left smiling!

We *all* need more joy in our lives, but this idea would be especially good to do for someone in the later years of grieving.

13. Create Support Systems for People

Once I saw a grown man cry.
"Now there goes a man with feeling!" said I.
He was strong, able, quite well-built,
With muscles, gray hair, and charm to the hilt.
I moved toward him slowly and said,
"What's wrong?"
The look he gave me was tear-filled and long.
"I cry for a child.
My grandchild has died."
So I sat beside him and
Two grown men cried.
    —Margaret H. Gerner, *For Bereaved Grandparents*

Empathy feels these thoughts: your hurt is in my heart, your loss is in my prayers, your sorrow is in my soul, and your tears are in my eyes.
    —William Arthur Ward
      (American writer, pastor, and teacher, 1921–1997)

Tears are often the telescope through which men see into heaven.
    —Anonymous

For most of us, going through a loss for the first time can be the loneliest time of our entire lives because we feel like *no one* really understands our pain. When we are able to find others who have traveled a similar path, we find that we are not alone, and that is one of the first steps to healing. Because grieving persons simply do not have the energy to find support groups on their own, one of the ways you can help them is to research and provide information on what is available in your community. It would mean even more if you or someone else they knew would attend with them, especially the first time.

Celebrate Traditions of Other Cultures to Work through the Grieving Process

There is a Buddhist tradition known in Japan as "1,000 Cranes." When someone is ill or grieving, the rest of the family or friends make one thousand origami cranes. Then they are attached to string and wire so that they hang above someone's bed. You often see these in hospital rooms in Tokyo. The person who shared this tradition with me said that with each crane that is made, the creator says this prayer, "I wish for wholeness, health, and happiness for the whole family." What a lovely, visual way to make their prayers and caring known.

After 9/11 Amy Segami, a Chinese American, sent the following message to friends to come together to mourn and then move on as her family tradition dictates:

> Another sunrise . . . In ancient China, one was allowed to grieve officially for one hundred days. In the aftermath of the turmoil and chaos of September 11, we were told to go back to our "normal" life immediately. However, the reality set in. My heart was heavy. My eyes hurt from weeping. Let's together look for ways to transform tragedy and sorrow into improvement for humanity, whether it's doing research on hydrogen fuel or increasing airline security. Let's help find a way. This is America! I miss seeing many of you. Would you like to join me for a sunrise gathering just to appreciate the beauty of nature and friendship and the beginning of another new day of hope? Meet on Sunday, September 30, from 6:33 A.M. until 9:28 A.M. Foster Beach at Lake Michigan, Chicago, East of the parking lot, under Segami's American Flag. Afterward we will go for Dim Sum."

The next week, she sent another invitation: "Before the sunset . . . There must be a way: for those who could not make it before the sunrise, fortunately, there is the sunset. As you may recall, I arranged a sunrise gathering two weeks ago. It was a beautiful sunrise. After the Dim Sum Brunch, we all felt much better. Confucius was right: We are born to eat! In ancient China, not only was one allowed to grieve officially for one hundred days, one also got together with relatives and friends to share a banquet. The point was to soothe the soul, pay tribute to life, and make plans for the future. Normally, you are invited to a ten-course banquet if you are part of the family circle. Join me for a ten-course banquet at Phoenix Restaurant in Chicago's Chinatown as part of the grieving tradition.

Arthur Gershowitz shares the grieving process proscribed by the Jewish religion and how important other people are in carrying it through:

When a parent, spouse, or sibling dies, there is a one-week period of mourning (called "shiva") in which one "sits" shiva. During this time one doesn't leave the home where you are sitting shiva. The community (i.e. your friends, and others interested in your welfare) visit during the week bringing food and a receptive ear to listen to whatever it is you want to talk about. Conversation ranges from memories of the deceased to anything people happen to want to talk about (sometimes one has to take a break, even from grieving). After shiva is over, it is followed by the very symbolic act of leaving the house and taking a walk around the block. This represents your re-entry into the world. Even though your heart isn't in it, it is necessary to force oneself back into life. This doesn't mean grieving is over.

For the first month after the death of a spouse or sibling one says Kaddish every day. This is a prayer that requires ten people be present to recite, so again it calls the community together to help. For a parent, one says Kaddish every day for eleven months (I did this when my father died three years ago). There are other customs observed during the mourning period, but it would take a book for me to go over them. The mourning process is not something that one does for a couple of days. The reality is that when it is for someone close, the mourning never really stops, it simply becomes a part of you. This isn't to say that one is grief stricken around the clock forever. It's important to re-enter the world and to enjoy life. But one never forgets the departed. And the process of re-entry can be difficult and time consuming and will vary from person to person.

Begin a Support Group

Darla Arni shared how she and her husband found solace in starting a support group in their community. This is something you could also do for a family member, colleague, or friend:

Many years ago, just six months after my husband Paul and I were married, we went through a terrible year of change and loss. On June 16th, just days before Father's Day, my father died suddenly, on September 1st Paul's mother died after a long fight with emphysema, and after finding out we were pregnant in October, we lost the baby in January due to genetic problems. It was the lowest point of my life. It seemed as if God and the whole world was against us, and I struggled to find ways to cope and find something positive in everything that was happening to us.

First, just to get through the day I kept myself busy with anything that would allow me not to think. As soon as I got home from a full day of teaching, I began doing crossword puzzles. In fact, I became obsessed with crossword puzzles! As long as I was concentrating on them, my brain wasn't free to worry, blame, or rehash everything that was eating me up inside. But that was a temporary fix. It wasn't until my doctor told us about Compassionate Friends that things began to change.

Compassionate Friends is a nationwide support group/network for those who have lost children. Unfortunately, there was no group within one hundred miles of where we live. Instead, we contacted the minister who married us and began talking to her about our loss and also shared with her the existence of the Compassionate Friends group. The more we met, the more we decided that there were others like us who could benefit from such a group and, along with our minister, we helped charter a Compassionate Friends chapter for our area.

Since that time, the group has grown and now has regular meetings, a support newsletter, and regular activities for those who have experienced such loss. While we haven't actively attended meetings for the past six years, we still support the group monetarily and spread the word to anyone who needs to hear its message. The moral of this experience is that if we had kept our hurt inside and not shared how we felt and that we needed help, not only would our lives have suffered, but we would never have had the opportunity to bring such an organization into being so others could be helped. This was our positive that came out of loss!

Encourage the Grieving Person to Try Something New

One of the ways we can help people to move on with their lives is to encourage them to do something different than they have ever done before. It may be to sign up for a class or try a new sport or join a new group. As soon as they take this step, as difficult as it is, it represents going forward in a new life. There is a fine line between encouraging and forcing, and it is important to respect the feelings of the bereaved person. They must feel ready to take this step. However, if you walk alongside them, you will make it much easier, and the first time they reach out of themselves will be a major victory and a real reason for celebration!

A year after Charlie died, I was at our home in Sarasota, Florida, in July and August to finish writing a new book. I spent at least an hour a day walking our beautiful beach. This special time helped heal some of my loneliness as I watched how the beach and the water were different every day and yet as constant as we know God's love is for us. The third week I was there, my mother, sister, niece, and brother came to visit. Bruce is a marine biologist and a college professor, and he loves the outdoors. One day he rented a kayak and took it out by himself into the bay.

As he told us about it, I was intrigued. I had never been in a kayak, and all of a sudden, I realized that I *could* try some new things I had never done before. Charlie had had most of his adventures before we were married, and because money was tight and we had three children, we spent most of our recreational time doing things for them. I told Bruce that if he would take me out the next day, I would pay for the kayak! We rented a two-man sit-on-top kayak for the day, and I loved it. We paddled through a bird sanctuary on the bay side and down the shore where we could see the beautiful homes and boats of the residents. Then we took the boat over to the gulf side on our beach. We had not been out five minutes when right into us swam a school of dolphins! Bruce jumped out of the boat to swim with them, and I paddled right alongside them. I decided that this was a special sign just for me.

The next day Bruce came with me, and I bought a two man sit-on-top kayak, complete with all the accessories, including a small cart on wheels so that I can handle it myself. The boat I chose was red, orange, and yellow, and the design was called "Sunrise." As a symbol of what is happening in my life, I have named it "New Beginnings!" I will always be grateful to my brother for encouraging me and guiding me to do something completely new in my life!

Create a Ritual of Support

In her book, *Cancer Has Its Privileges,* Christine Clifford Beckwith shares an idea from a woman from New Orleans who was diagnosed with Stage IV breast cancer. She wanted to focus on the gifts rather than the pain of each new day and wanted a visual representation that friends and family could participate in. She decided to collect marbles, so she asked all her family and friends to contribute to her collection.

Each morning she would put one clear glass marble in a beautiful blue glass bowl. It represented her hopes for the day: "sunshine, afternoon tea, a warm fire, or just feeling well enough to take a stroll around the house." Each night a colored marble placed in the bowl would represent her thanks: "a visit from a friend, a get-well message, or the healing touch of a hug."

She had no idea what a huge role these little marbles would play in her healing. She got them from as far away as Cairo, Egypt, and as near as the child across the street. Since many friends and family participated in the ritual, too, they learned to appreciate the small blessings of every day that so often go unnoticed. And Val has learned to give thanks for the greatest gift of all, everyday *life.*

Be Aware of the Stages of Grieving As You Help Another

A nurse shares the stages of her grief upon losing her dog, Jagger:

After six-and-a-half years, my dog, Jagger, is gone. He was part yellow Lab and part mastiff which made a very unique and interesting combination. Everyone feels that their pet is special but Jagger was more than special to me. Just as you can have a soul mate, I believe that you can have a soul pet and he was my soul dog. When he left, he took a piece of my heart with him that I must learn to live without or fill up somehow.

First, I had to come to terms with the fact that he was gone, and I went through the grieving process of denial. I kept his food, toys, and bowls, and his leash hung in the kitchen. This made me feel every day as though he were still there but was not helping me to get over my loss. He was allowed on one living room couch, and I found myself sitting there a lot, waiting for him to snuggle his face up to mine. Next, anger overwhelmed me. I could not stand to see anyone walking their dog without seething inside. It seemed so unfair that they had a dog and now I did not. I yelled at God for letting my dog go. I blamed many people, including myself. This is not a good nor healthy stage of grieving, but it is part of the healing process.

Moving on to the next stage, I tried to bargain with God. I wanted a miracle to happen and was willing to pay any price. Bargaining does not work, but it is a distraction at least and makes you look inside yourself. Then, I was deeply depressed over my loss.

As a nurse, I have noticed that everyone has their own timetable of grieving, and sometimes that is difficult for others around them to accept. I was avoiding my friends who wanted to be there for me. Depression does that to you. You need people the most when you are depressed, but when you are depressed, it is very hard to reach out to others. I preferred to sit and cry by myself in a dark room. The outside seemed too bright and cheery and active for me. I spent a week sitting, crying, and not eating. It is fine to have a "Pity Party" for five days or so, but you cannot get over a loss by taking up residence in "Pity City." Also, not eating helps to push you further into depression.

After forcing myself to meet friends for lunch, I began to feel less depressed. It was an effort at first, and I faked feeling fine. It took a lot of energy to fake being happy when I had a broken heart. I continued forcing myself to socialize and slowly did begin to feel better. Friends and family are an excellent source of comfort, but you have to reach out and accept it. Planning social events with people helped me become distracted over my loss. Some people may call this "getting on with life."

It is difficult to leave the comfort of depression to move onto the last stage of grieving, which is acceptance. Time also has a way of helping us to get over grieving. I don't think we get over grieving as much as we learn to fill the void left by the deceased. Acceptance teaches you to remember the good times without becoming deeply depressed or angry. Acceptance can be accomplished or enhanced by joining a grieving group in your community. Just call the local hospital to discover the nearest grieving group in your area.

I am in the process of volunteering at the Seeing Eye Dog Center in my area to help walk the dogs because I feel this is what will help me the most. People will have a lot of ideas to help you, if you ask them. Not all of their ideas will work, but you won't know until you try. Find a new interest or take a class in something you are interested in. It was suggested that I get a puppy, but this was not the answer for me. Your heart will let you know what works for you. Don't give up if one thing does not work. Check out alternative possibilities. One thing that helped me was realizing that only I could take that first step in reaching out to people and finding things to occupy my time and heal my broken heart. Jagger will always hold an important section of my heart, but I am opening up my heart to healthy and healing experiences.

Note: Dr. Elisabeth Kübler-Ross coined the five stages of grief (denial, anger, bargaining, depression, and acceptance) in her first book, *On Death and Dying,* in 1969.

14. Create Traditions That Keep the Memory of a Loved One Alive

To live in the hearts we leave behind is not to die.
—Thomas Campbell

The monument of a great man is not of granite or marble or bronze. It consists of his goodness, his deeds, his love, and his compassion.
—Alfred Montapert

One of the best ways to help someone overcome one's grieving is to find something to do in memory of a loved one or a friend. And the best gift we can give a grieving friend is to talk about that person, to keep his or her memory alive through new traditions created just for this difficult time. When our second child died at Christmastime, I thought I could never survive, but the gifts of some wonderful friends made that time just a little bit easier.

You will read some touching stories in this section about how both parents and friends have found precious ways to remember those who have passed on. My prayer is that they will trigger ideas for you so that when someone you know and love is grieving, you will not feel so helpless. No matter how strong one's faith, the desolation and loneliness of never again being able to hold and touch someone we love can only be healed by the gifts of love from others around us and from the assurance that that person's life *did* make a difference. We can help by honoring their memories. Please remember as you read these difficult stories not to focus on the tragedies that occurred but rather to celebrate the legacy of love these beloved ones have left behind. Use the memorial gift ideas as ways to help others who are grieving remember their loved ones in visible and concrete ways.

Dedicate a Book on the Child's Birthday

The David Schulz family of Downers Grove, Illinois, gave us a most precious gift when our son died. Each year, on December 21, Gavin's birthday, they picked a special book that would be appropriate for his age and dedicated it to our town library in his memory. Each book has a bookplate inside with a memorial note about him. Even today, over thirty years later, I love to go to the library and check out those books. I know that each child who reads them will think about our little boy! On the year he would have been twenty-one, I received a letter from them saying, "Now that Gavin is an adult in heaven, we have decided to donate money to Habitat for Humanity in his name so that a family on earth can be helped in his memory." Not only did they acknowledge his life, but they kept his memory alive over all those years in dear and meaningful ways.

Adopt a Child in Another Country in Memory of the Deceased

As a family we, too, decided to do something in Gavin's memory. Through Compassion International we have sponsored two little boys in Colombia, one from age seven until he graduated from high school, and we are presently sponsoring another young man who is now eleven. We keep their pictures with our other family pictures and write to them regularly. It has been a great comfort to know that even though we can't do anything materially for our son any longer, we can help another young man to have a better life here. As a friend or family member, you might decide to do this for the grieving person in honor of their loved one.

Give a Single White Rose

Several years ago, I wrote a story about someone who helped keep our son's memory alive.

In 1971 I faced the most difficult experience of my life, one which has changed me forever. I had grown up in a small town in Iowa where families were the center of our lives. I loved dolls and baby-sitting, and I could hardly wait to be a mother! I even became a high school English teacher because I loved working with young people. In 1965 I graduated from the University of

Kansas and began teaching in LaGrange, Illinois. In 1966 I married a wonderful man named Charlie, and on April 2, 1969, we were blessed with our first child, Garrett Wayne Glanz.

I felt in control of my life and filled with thanksgiving and anticipation for the future. We had saved all of my teaching paychecks and were able to put a down payment on a small English cottage in Western Springs, Illinois. Charlie was doing well in his work at the Chicago Tribune, and I found out I was pregnant again in early 1971. We were ecstatic!

I had a perfectly normal pregnancy, teaching adult swimming two mornings a week at the YMCA, and loving each moment of teaching our little son, Garrett, about our beautiful world. Our second child was due January 3, 1972. On December 20, I began having labor pains in the night, so we took Garrett to the neighbor's and went to the hospital. Since I was nearly fully dilated and only two-and-a-half weeks early, the doctor induced labor, and our second child, Gavin Ward Glanz, was born at 4:45 p.m. on December 21, 1971. We spent the evening calling all our family and friends to share our joy, and both of us tried to get a much-needed good night's sleep. The next day the nightmare began!

When our pediatrician and personal friend, Dr. Allen, walked into my room early the next morning, I immediately knew something was wrong. With great difficulty, he told us that he thought our baby son had a congenital heart defect and they were taking him by ambulance to Cook County Children's Hospital to the best pediatric cardiologist in the area. However, he said not to give up hope because often open-heart surgery could be performed and the child could be fine, so Charlie followed the ambulance, and I began the awful waiting.

Later that afternoon, Charlie called to tell me that our baby had died. The problem turned out to be with his lungs, and there was no way they could have saved him even though he weighed more than seven pounds. He was buried on Christmas Eve.

I know that never again in my life will I feel so helpless and so completely empty—I would have traded my life for his in an instant! Because none of our family or friends ever got to know him, hold him, or even see his picture (the hospital didn't take one), they had a difficult time relating to our grief, and although they were sad for us, they really felt little connection to our son.

As a result, much of the time Charlie and I felt alone in our deep love for him and in the terrible loss of being able to watch him grow and become an adult.

I tried to go on with my life, especially since we had a young son who needed me; however, there were days when I didn't think I could make it through even the morning, so deep was my grief and sense of loss. About that time someone gave me a copy of a book that has forever influenced my life and helped make my recovery possible. It was by Jess Lair, a wonderful Christian man, who talked about living five minutes at a time. Many days I could not face even another hour, but I could always get through five minutes, and I consciously held onto that and my faith in a loving God as a means of survival. That was one of the beautiful lessons I learned through all my pain—to be fully in the present and to treasure every minute of every day. However, I still struggled with people's reluctance to talk about our son, their lack of memories of him, and the terrible void there was in my life.

On December 21,1972, the day which would have been Gavin's first birthday, the doorbell rang, and there at the doorstep was a delivery man from the florist. He had a small bud vase holding one single white rose. With it was a card from some very dear friends that read, "This is in memory of a very special life, one which we know will make a difference in this world—Gavin Ward Glanz." And each year for many years on December 21, that single white rose has arrived on our doorstep—a symbol that someone in this often indifferent, rushed world of ours does remember the life of our little boy.

And they were right—he has made a difference in this world through me, the person I have become because of his life and death, and the abiding message of hope I am able to share with others as I speak all over the world.

A beautiful postscript to this story is that on May 17, 1998, our first little grandson was born, and what did they name him? Gavin William Glanz. How very blessed we are! Our son lives on through this precious gift of new life, and we will always celebrate our new little Gavin's birthday with one single white rose.
© Barbara Glanz Communications, Inc., 1999. All rights reserved.

This story exemplifies how a simple gift of remembrance and caring can help heal a broken heart and become a family tradition.

Kathy Pacey has a friend who sends her and her husband one white rose in their only child Tommy's memory each Easter. She addresses it to "Tommy's Mommy and Daddy." Kathy says, "It means so much to have those little special things." The givers of these single white roses will never fully know the difference they have made in two people's lives.

Light a Candle Every Year at the Same Time

The Compassionate Friends, an organization for anyone who has lost a child, grandchild, godchild, brother, sister, niece, or nephew, has a worldwide candle-lighting ceremony the second Sunday of December at 7:00 P.M. (your local time) in memory of all the children who have died. Everyone lights their candles, whether in their homes or at the Children's Memorial Day meetings held in various cities across the country. At these organized ceremonies they also light five special candles for the survivors in the lost children's honor: one candle for their grief, one candle for their courage, one for their memories, one for their love, and finally, one for hope.

When Belle Fangmeyer heard about this, she thought of her niece who had passed away this year. She bought two identical candle holders and had the date of the candle-lighting ceremony engraved on each one. She gave one to her sister-in-law, the mother of Lisa Marie who died, and she kept one herself. They lit their candles together for the first time on December 7, 2004. Then Belle told her, "Wherever you are next year on December 7, I'll call and we'll light our candles together in memory of Lisa Marie." What a moving way to remember a loved child!

Light Luminaria Bags in the Person's Memory

A woman from Naperville, Illinois, whose teenage son Jason was killed in a boating accident, shared how she keeps his memory alive in a beautiful way. Every year at the beginning of December, she buys special luminaria bags. Then she sends one to each of her son's friends and family who are scattered all over the country.

She asks them to decorate the bag in a way that helps them remember their friend Jason. Sometimes they attach a photograph taken with Jason, others write letters of remembrance or poems, and some even make a picture or collage of things they loved to do together. They then send the decorated bags back to her, and on Christmas Eve she puts them around Jason's grave at the cemetery.

It becomes a healing for them all—a special celebration of Jason and what his life meant to each of them.

This woman says that she receives close to one hundred bags each year from many people who knew Jason. She invites anyone who wants to come to the cemetery on Christmas Eve night where they each light a candle as music is played, and they sing "Silent Night." One year the young woman who had received both Jason's lungs sent a luminaria bag to thank Jason for giving her life back to her. Jason's mother and his ten-year-old brother, Corey, make a copy of each of the bags and puts the pictures in a binder as an ongoing memory. (©Barbara Glanz Communications, Inc. Reprinted with permission from *Care Packages for the Home.*)

The holidays are the most difficult times for those of us who have lost a loved one. Ignoring our pain and trying to make things "normal" is not helpful. The real gift you can give to us is to share our memories and good times. We need to know that the life of our loved ones has made a difference in this world.

Develop Travel Rituals

Because their son had always loved traveling, the first family trip a bereaved family took after his death was devastating. However, their daughter needed this time away for her healing, so they decided to create some rituals around travel that can help any family who has had a loss.

The mother writes, "If possible, choose a new destination that is not so much a part of your loved one's life. Eventually we have been able to return to the Smokies and Disney World, but that first summer even King's Island was too painful. We chose Michigan instead, a place Jon had never visited with us. Expect the pain of leaving and returning. For our family, it worked well to develop a ritual as a part of each trip. We asked Jon to travel with us as our guardian angel at the beginning of the trip, and we always brought back a rock, shell, or other item to put on his grave at our trip's end and, if possible, stopped at the cemetery before returning home. Know that it won't always be this painful and look for signs of your loved one's presence with you wherever you go. Look for rainbows, pennies from heaven, and butterflies."

15. Find a Concrete Way to Remember the Person Who Died

The journey from grief to hope
Does not happen swiftly.
But it happens,
If you will let your heart
Ride along.
  —Sascha Wagner, *Wintersun*

The day will come when my body will lie upon a white sheet neatly tucked under four corners of a mattress located in a hospital; busily occupied with the living and the dying. At a certain moment a doctor will determine that my brain has ceased to function and that, for all intents and purposes, my life has stopped. When that happens, do not attempt to instill artificial life into my body by the use of a machine. And don't call this my deathbed. Let it be called the bed of life, and let my body be taken from it to help others lead fuller lives. Give my sight to the man who has never seen a sunrise, a baby's face or love in the eyes of a woman. Give my heart to a person whose own heart has caused nothing but endless days of pain. Give my blood to the teenager who was pulled from the wreckage of his car, so that he might live to see his grandchildren play. Give my kidneys to the one who depends on a machine to exist from week to week. Take my bones, every muscle, every fiber and nerve in my body and find a way to make a crippled child walk. Explore every corner of my brain. Take my cells, if necessary, and let them grow so that, someday a speechless boy will shout at the crack of a bat and a deaf girl will hear the sound of rain against her window. Burn what is left of me and scatter the ashes to the winds to help the flowers grow. If you must bury something, let it be my faults, my weakness and

all prejudice against my fellow man. Give my sins to the devil. Give my soul to God. If, by chance, you wish to remember me, do it with a kind deed or word to someone who needs you. If you do all I have asked, I will live forever.
—Robert N. Test, "To Remember Me"

It helps all of us who are grieving to have some *concrete* ways of remembering the person or the life we have lost. These memorials help us to face the reality of the loss as well as to honor the good times. They can become a symbol of acceptance and a way of letting go and moving on while still acknowledging and honoring the joy of the past.

Angelo and Linda Tomasello shared some of the ways friends and family keep their daughter Celeste's memory alive:

- Celeste has a star named for her through the International Star Registry, www.celestis.com.
- Celeste's friends made her a quilt using scanned photos transferred to fabric.
- A page was dedicated to Celeste in her yearbook.
- A dance was held in her honor and the funds raised started a scholarship for a high school senior who demonstrated Celeste's qualities.
- Friends came together to make decorations for the Christmas tree at her grave.

Here are a few more ideas to put to use:
- Start a scrapbook and include in it photographs of the person during happy moments in life.
- Build a memory box and fill it with mementoes: letters, poems, pictures, etc.
- Plant a tree or create a garden with flowers she or he especially liked.
- Create a family genealogy.
- Donate time to that person's favorite cause.
- Help that person's family create space within a room for photos and meaningful objects.

- Fund a cause held dear by that loved one.
- Start a scholarship program in that person's name.
- Contribute financially to any one of the arts that may have held a special place in that person's life.

Make a Charm Bracelet

One woman told me that when her daughter died of cancer, she created a charm bracelet containing special memories of her daughter and all the things she loved.

Purchase a Memorial Brick

This idea is one that has many variations. However, many groups now are using building markers as fundraisers and memorials to those we love. Several friends of mine donated money for a stone with our son's name engraved on it at the new headquarters of my sorority, Gamma Phi Beta, in Denver, Colorado. Although the story below is written by the mother of a child who died, keep in mind that this is also something you could do for a friend or colleague, as well as a family member.

Kathy Pacey, Tommy's loving mommy from Woodridge, Illinois, tells about a memorial brick that was purchased in memory of several children, including Tommy:

On Sunday, July 11, the Downers Grove Public Library dedicated the brick walkway I had told you about last year. As a fundraiser, you could buy a single or double brick and have it engraved with your message. Tim and I pitched in with Dave and Karen Putnam, John and Sue Freeman, and Mike and Maribeth Kavanaugh to buy a double brick bearing all of our sons' names. What follows is my "brick story." I hope you like it!

"One Paver Stone, Four Sons, and the Mothers Who Love Them"
Every brick does indeed have a story, though I doubt there is another quite like ours. Our brick is not simply in memory of a special occasion or person. Our brick represents so much more. It's about beginnings and endings; joys and sorrows; loss and survival; mothers and sons; the young and the old; the past and the future; love of this world and the next. Our brick represents the yin and yang of life itself.

It represents the beginning of our grief journey at the ending of our son's lives; the joy of friendship borne of life's greatest sorrow; the loss of four sons and survival of four mothers; the young preceding the old in death; honoring the past while preparing for the future; our love shared in this world and extending into the next. Our brick represents a bond formed between four women from four decades of life who see no differences, only commonalities in their relationship with one another.

When one reads our brick, "Forever Loved, Ken Putnam, William Kavanaugh, John Freeman, Tommy Pacey," one might think these boys were related, or were friends, or perhaps died tragically together. Our children are not related, nor were they friends. Our children did not live together, nor did they die together. In fact, our sons were total strangers in this life, but within eight months they passed, one by one, from this life into the next.

In less than eight months' time we four mothers had experienced the unthinkable—the most difficult loss imaginable: the death of a child. We all attend a monthly grief support group, Bereaved Parents of the USA. On the first Friday of each month, one has a good chance of finding us "Four Musketeers" at Redeemer Lutheran Church in Hinsdale, Illinois, from 8 P.M. until 10 P.M. We all became acquainted through this group, and over the years our friendship has blossomed. We support each other, not just once a month, but on a daily basis, being especially attentive on those very difficult anniversary dates.

We're fond of saying that our children are hanging out in heaven together as a result of our friendship here on earth, but who's to say—perhaps it was *they* who orchestrated our friendship down here from up above. Either way, it's a comforting thought.

Thank you for giving us a "concrete" memorial to our four very precious beloved children. Thank you for taking an interest in our story—for giving us a chance to tell it, and for listening. You have no idea what a gift that is to a bereaved parent, particularly as the years roll by. Please, the next time you meet a bereaved parent, or see one you already know, *do* mention their child. It's music to our ears!

Host a Conference in Their Memory

Denise White writes about what her sons did to memorialize their brother Shawn: "Less than six months after his passing, even though they live great distances away, our other sons (those who grew up with Shawn) talked about how they could pass on the heritage and legacy of Shawn. They formed a committee and hosted a conference in memory of Shawn and my brother, Dirk. They did a fantastic job bringing together young men and boys to discuss risk-taking behaviors, family values, health issues, and the importance of God in their lives. It was yet another way for them to pass on the values of Shawn to the next generation. Michael and I are very proud of them."

Plant a Butterfly Garden

The butterfly, a beautiful symbol of hope and rebirth, is a special reminder of our loved ones who are gone. Since I speak on "Regenerating Spirit in the Workplace," I have always used a butterfly as my logo. However, it means much more to me than just a logo as it represents the comfort of knowing that all the dear ones in my life who have passed away are just fine!

Think about planting a special garden that will attract butterflies to be a constant reminder of the one you loved. If you have a small piece of ground (as small as 5' x 5'), you can purchase a shaker of wild flower or butterfly flower seeds. Rough up the ground or turn under existing grass, rake the soil slightly and scatter the flower seeds thickly throughout the area. Water daily, and in a few weeks you will have a beautiful garden that will attract various types of butterflies. The best part is *you don't have to weed it!*

The other advantage to this type of garden is that you need only shake the seeds down into the soil during the winter months and when spring arrives the next year, you will already have a vast majority of flowers returning. The mix is usually full of both perennials and biannuals, so you only need to replace the annual seeds in the garden. If you have some large leaf plants (perhaps on the border of the garden), your butterfly friends will lay eggs and you will find caterpillars munching on the leaves in no time at all! What a precious and beautiful reminder it will be of those who are gone.

Plant Flowers, Bulbs, or a Bush

When a woman's adopted daughter was killed in a car accident, friends gave her bulbs to plant and went together and bought a bird bath so that she could create "April's garden." She says it gives her great comfort as she sees the flowers come back each and every year. They remind her of hope, new life, and the love of friends.

Tom Burley from Seattle shares what his company did when his mother died: "Patricia S. Burley, 'Mom,' was, in every way, the consummate mother to me and my sisters and the most generous and playful of grandmothers to my sons. A greater mother a son never had! She was also a gardener-extraordinaire, planting scores of flowers and caring for her many prize rhododendrons. I thought her gardens were a little preview of heaven. She died of a brain tumor in July 1994. To show support and love for me, the Executive Council (President and Vice Presidents) of CRISTA Ministries, my employer, gave me a beautiful rhododendron bush to plant in my garden as a living reminder of Mom. I think of her, and the graciousness of the givers, everytime I walk by that rhody."

Oralee Thompson shared how gifts of plants have been a blessing to her: "When Ellen died, my sister-in-law gave me a pot of forget-me-not plants to plant in Ellen's honor, so they come up every year as a remembrance of her. I then gave some to each one of her friends that helped with the family lunch I had at my house after the wake. I found out later that they were one of Ellen's favorite spring flowers and she had planted several of them the spring before she died at her Michigan home. Since they come up every year, they have now really taken over her garden in Michigan! Ellen and I went to Morton Arboretum before she died and walked through in both the spring and the fall, just reflecting and enjoying God's creation. It makes me feel so close to her whenever I go back there to enjoy the park."

Plant a "Memory Tree"

A mother shares how she memorialized her precious little daughter:

> When my infant daughter died shortly after birth, I determined I would do something positive in life to remind me of her. At every home I have lived, I have planted a pink dogwood tree in

memory of her. When I have sold my homes, I have told the new owner that it is a "memory tree," and I know that the tree will bring them great joy each spring when it blooms. I have enjoyed watching these trees grow over the years and the new owners enjoy them. The ones I have planted are all still there at each of my homes and doing well.

Most recently in the fall of 2002, my new husband and I purchased my dream, a log home on ten acres, in the country, surrounded my beautiful trees and woods.

Last spring, I planted the traditional pink dogwood in memory of my daughter, Jennifer. I took it one step further this time, since we plan on retiring in this home, God willing, and I am planting an entire garden, full of perennials, an angel statue and bird bath. It is lovely and a precious "memory place" for our little Jennifer.

Design a Tribute Calendar

Carol Copeland Thomas shares the tribute she and her friends created to memorialize their sons:

"Four Mothers with Love" is a millennium tribute calendar dedicated to our children who lost their lives between June and July of 1997. Rather then silently suffering their deaths, we have decided to celebrate the gifts that they brought to the world. All were in school pursuing their life dreams. All made mistakes like other young people on their journey to adulthood. All had a passion for being the best and developing to their fullest potential. All had reached a certain level in life where their real purpose was being fulfilled. All believed in the awesome power and grace of God.

The calendar is filled with family stories and pictures of each young man and describes the personal legacies that they left behind. Important Black history dates and events are highlighted each month, and you will also find Student Safety Month information that will be observed during the month of June 2000. There is something for everyone in "Four Mothers with Love!"

Unlike other stories about troubled African American young males prone to violence, excessive drugs, and social unrest, it was important for us to tell the other side of the story so often withheld from newspapers and television reports. Our sons were not troubled, managed to stay away from criminal activity, and in many ways were role models for others. Their loss leaves an empty hole for humanity to fill with the decency and compassion that they shared with others. Their smiles, jokes, teen pranks, and intellect will be sorely missed. Their love for their families has kept us from falling apart.

These beautiful women have found a way not only to memorialize their sons but also to help others in their memory. We give the most precious gift when we use our pain to help others.

Participate in a Walk

Jim Flynn, a "chosen" family member did something very special in Charlie's memory:

> Barb, I know there is nothing I could say that would fill the void of your loss. I would, however, like to do something in your honor and in memory of Charlie, in hopes that it might lift your spirits.
>
> Each year there is a "Walk for Life" held in Tucson to raise funds in the fight against cancer. During the walk, luminaries are lit honoring people who are currently fighting cancer and honoring people who have given their lives fighting against cancer. Donations are made in honor of each person for whom a luminary is lighted and teams of people walk to raise additional funds from sponsors and individual donors. During the walk, when all the luminaries are lighted, a special ceremony is held in the darkness (except for the luminaries) and the litany of names from the luminaries is read. It is truly a moving experience.
>
> This year, Diana and I will light luminaries for you and Charlie, and we'll walk and make our donation in honor of you both. We'll do this in the hopes that a good cure for cancer will be found in the near future, to save others from the pain and loss you have experienced.

What a remarkable way to memorialize a loved one!

Another speaker friend, John Blumberg, donated a speech to a local Christian organization while Charlie was ill, and as his "payment," he asked for prayers for my husband and me. I will never forget his generosity. Anything we can do in the name of the deceased or the grieving person is a most precious gift.

16. Share Your Learnings from a Loved One's Life

I Choose
To feel sorry for myself as a victim of life and death
OR
To help others to understand and grow through their grief

To complain that he abandoned me
OR
To appreciate the blessing he was in my life

To think sad thoughts of missing him
OR
To think happy thoughts remembering the years we shared

To see you critically stare at me . . . seeing if I measure up
OR
To feel you wonder at who is behind my deep blue eyes

To envy your social charm, confidence, and ability to find a
new love
OR
Be happy with who I am and find
      Warmth and
           Security
                In seeing "aloneness" as
                Just one of my choices
To call for love
OR
To be loving.
    —Cheryl Perlitz

When is it all right to cry?
Whenever we feel like it.
When is it all right to smile and laugh?
Whenever we feel like it.
When is it all right to feel guilty because we laugh or cry?
Never!
   —Terri Kelly

One of the ways I have found to heal is to share what I have learned as a result of my journey through grief. In fact, that is how this book came about! The legacy we can leave to those we have loved and lost is to make their lives count for something in the ways we now choose to live ours, and any service we can do for others as a result memorializes them and gives their lives meaning.

Do the Things on Your List *Now!*

Davis L. Fisher of Evanston, Illinois, shared what he learned from his brother's death:

A few years ago a voice deep inside was saying to me: "You're supposed to be doing something more." I didn't have time to listen to that voice, but I knew that things seemed out of sync. I felt that I was supposed to build on where I had been in my life and work, that I was to make some kind of major shift, but I told myself that that was silly, that I didn't have time to do something like that. Things were going well, it seemed. I was very involved in activities in both my personal and professional life. So I pushed that voice down.

And then it happened. My only sibling, brother Chuck, six years older than I, contracted cancer and after a long battle, died at the age of fifty-six. In going through his effects, I found a handwritten list of "Things I Wish I Had Done." Ooh, that hit hard. I wondered, "What kind of a list would I make?" Of course I could make a list . . . each of us could. Then I looked at Chuck's list more closely: "Wish I had traveled more. Wish I had married and had children. Wish I had read more for pleasure." It would have been much easier to accept if Chuck had written, "Wish I had flown to the moon," or "Wish I had won the lottery." But, no. What Chuck had written were things over which he had control. He just didn't get around to doing them because he was very busy.

This is not an indictment of brother Chuck; it is an indictment of our human condition today. We don't seem to take the time for the things that—on our deathbed—we are likely to say that we wish we had done.

What a gift Chuck gave me through the list he had made! I vowed that my deathbed list would not include the words, "I wish I had listened to that voice inside." Soon I plunged myself into discernment, followed by some bold steps. Today I am doing unique, innovative, and fulfilling work . . . with a passion.

Coming to me at the least expected time and place, this gift changed the course of my life. I am grateful that I was able to recognize Chuck's list as a gift. It makes me wonder how many gifts I may have received from others in the past and failed to recognize.

And I wonder something else: I am convinced that Chuck was not aware of the priceless gift he had given to me. Am I aware of the gifts that I may be giving to others? The giving and receiving of gifts—so powerful and often, so subtle.

©Davis L. Fisher, Moneytree Consulting, Evanston, Ill., 1989. Reprinted with permission.

When we are able to share lessons from the lives of those we loved, we not only help others but we also create a legacy in their name. How many of us make lists of things we want to do and then never make the time to do them? Like Davis, we need to remember Chuck!

Michael Poll shares an idea that encourages each of us reading this book to take the time to do something for our loved ones *now,* before we are gone:

After my grandmother, Lillian Adelson, died, the usual things occurred. There was a funeral and we sat Shiva (a customary mourning period for Jews). She was an extremely active member of her synagogue and many congregants came to visit with us during this time. In Judaism, a will is usually not read until one month after a person has died. Family members were mailed official documents, some from an attorney and some from the state of Maryland where she resided. The will stated various gifts that "Mom Mom" had selected for each of us to receive. Several months later, my aunt gave each of the grandchildren colorful bags that she had put together with the gifts inside. To our surprise, each bag had an envelope in it with "Mom Mom's" distinctive handwriting on it. It said, "A codicil will for Michael Poll from Lillian Adelson, to be opened one month after my death." "Mom Mom" had handwritten personal letters to each family member. Her personal words meant more to me than anything I could ever imagine, and I will treasure that letter forever. The person who did something special for me was the person who died!

Forgive Yourself When You Fail

Sometimes, out of our own discomfort, we let down the people that we love when they are in trouble. The important thing for us in healing is to forgive ourselves. Only then, can we reach out to others and find the joy that awaits us.

My friend, Joe Liss, told me this story:

Every guy has a best friend in their early teen years, right? Well, my friend was Todd. I met Todd when we entered junior high school, the seventh grade. He was smart, witty, funny, a very gentle young man. We became fast, inseparable friends. Every day after school we would do something together, whether it was play sports, play games, or study. We would always be at his house or mine.

Junior high school ended after the ninth grade. We were both going to attend the same high school. Prior to starting high school all students needed to get their routine physical. Todd's did not go well. They found he had a form of cancer that rarely forms in adolescents. It attacked growing, healthy cells. In a full-grown adult it would not have done that much damage because the cells were not growing. But in an adolescent it is devastating. Todd grew nine inches that summer. And the cancer grew exponentially. Todd's growth was quickly killing him. Todd was able to start high school but was hospitalized just after the start of our first semester. I could not visit him in the hospital. I did not have the strength to see my friend die. He passed away on Christmas Eve, 1971.

I was devastated. I had lost my friend and had not had the fortitude to be with him in his hour of need. I felt that I had let him and his family down. And I just didn't know how to deal with it.

Shortly after the funeral Todd's parents gave me some very old baseball cards. They know baseball is my passion. They had been given to Todd by his uncle, and his parents knew Todd would want me to have them. I never saw his parents again. I was too embarrassed to face them after not being there for Todd.

For years I would share those cards with various people. This would occur several times every year and everyone wanted to know how I got them. It always gave me an opportunity to share my friendship with Todd with new people. It also kept Todd's memory alive, and it kept the memory of having let him down an open sore.

I finally decided I had to close the book on my letting him down. I searched for his parents through the various contacts I knew and finally found them. I called up his mom on the phone in September 1998:

In a broken voice, "Hi, this is Joe Liss."

"Who?"

In a trembling and broken voice, "Joe Liss."

"JOE!"

After all these years we had finally connected! A few short moments of small talk is all I could handle and I told her I had to call her back. I sat down and wept. I don't remember ever having cried when Todd died. This was the first time I had cried for him. This was the first time I had actually allowed myself to mourn.

My wife, daughter, and I visited Todd's parents in December 1998. His mom and dad were just wonderful! They understood that not all people could handle such an experience. I was finally able to let go of those twenty-seven years of guilt. And they said it was wonderful to visit again. They didn't have opportunities to talk about Todd with people who knew him, let alone one of his best friends. We discussed what Todd might have done for a career, what kind of girls he would have liked, what his family may have been like. We experienced lots of joy and lots of tears.

©Joe Liss, 1998. All rights reserved. Reprinted with permission.

Give Away Your Angel Pin, Even If You Don't Feel Like It

My friend Lynn Durham, from New England, tells about her initial reluctance to share her angel pin and the resulting joy she found when she listened to a still, small voice that she really didn't want to hear:

I was at a conference, and perched on my shoulder was a beautiful gold pin. At first glance it looked like an eagle, but it was a beautiful angel, wings outstretched, a unique design, unlike any I have ever seen before or since. There's a little story how it came to be there. My sister's friend was wearing it originally. My sister tells me she said, "That pin is great, where did you find it? I'd like to buy one for my sister. She loves angels." Her friend took it off and gave it to my sister to give to me. Wow! And I was blessed with this lovely gift.

At the break, a woman came up to me and said, "That pin is great, where did you find it? I'd like to buy one for my sister. She loves angels." And then I heard a small voice say, "Give her the pin." So naturally, I said to myself, "No, this was given to me," and I heard again, "Give her the pin." So of course, I told myself, "No, what would Irene's friend think if I just gave it away?" Once more I heard, "Give her the pin." And I thought, "It's a very unusual pin, how could I find another?" And I heard louder, *"Give her the pin!"* With a cringe I took it off and said out loud to the woman, "Here, give this to your sister."

She was surprised at first and asked me if I was serious. I said, "Yes." When she said, "Are you sure?" I thought, "This is my opportunity to get it back!" and out of my mouth popped, "Yes." Then she said, "This is so wonderful. You'll never know what this will mean to her. She is dying of cancer."

Hmmmmm . . . After hearing those words and regretting my own reluctance, I decided to tell her what I just told you. That made the pin even more meaningful to her and her sister, so finally, I released the pin with love.

I believe things not only come to us, but are supposed to pass through us to get to where they need to go. Maybe this includes more than things—maybe people come into our lives and go on, blessed by our encounter, and they, too, are to be released in love. Life is a circle. Things are not just going back and forth, but around and around, and we play our part in moving things on in this dance of life. Are you ready to go with the flow? Are you listening to the small voice (or maybe not so small)? Do you say *"no!"* or *"yes!"*?

©Lynn Durham. Reprinted with permission.

It Is Never Too Late to Send a Note

A woman tells about wanting to write to the family of a doctor who treated her with great caring:

Some time ago I went to have a tattoo removed from my left buttock. The doctor dermabrased it and left me with a gaping open wound that covered one whole side. I couldn't stand the pain and called my family physician who agreed to see me. He took one look at me and sent me to a plastic surgeon. I was waiting in this plastic surgeon's examining room, and when he came in, the first thing he asked me was, "Are you on any pain medication?" He saw me every day for four days and on the fourth day asked me, "Do you have anyone to take care of your children (I had two toddlers) if you needed to go into the hospital?" Can you imagine? He was one of the most caring doctors I have ever known.

He saw me every day in the hospital. I had a nurse who didn't wait for the pain medication to take effect before she put ointment on me. I mentioned it to this plastic surgeon when he came in. I don't remember saying it angrily, I just was in pain. He came to see me that day before he left the hospital and said I was not to worry—that particular nurse would not be taking care of me again.

I recently read in the paper that this plastic surgeon passed away at age fifty-three. I immediately thought to send his wife a message about how much his caring had meant to me. I knew he didn't just care about me; the hospital nurses knew how wonderful he was, and in fact, the only day he didn't see me in the hospital was because he was home for his child's birthday. He said if I needed him that day, though, to let the nurses know, and they would reach him. Well, I mentioned to a friend that I was going to write a letter to his wife, and she made me feel like it wasn't such a great idea, so I have not written it. Your message yesterday made me rethink that. I need to trust my gut instincts more too. Thanks again, Barbara. I will write that letter!

Later I received the following e-mail:

Hi, Barbara,

Well, I wanted to let you know the outcome of my letter to the doctor's wife. I did indeed go with my gut (although it took a while), and I sent the doctor's wife a letter about my experience. I was so elated and relieved when she wrote back to thank me for taking the time to write and said that the note sounded just like her Kal and that that was the reason he was in private practice—so that he could practice medicine the way he thought is *should* be practiced. She thanked me for sharing the story with her and her family. I was *so glad* to know that my letter didn't cause her undue pain.

Thanks again for your presentation. It helped me to think of what I needed to do, not what someone else thought I should do.

Conclusion

One afternoon when he was very sick, my grandfather spoke to me of death and told me that he was dying (I was seven years old). "What does this mean, Grandpa?" I asked, worried and anxious.

"I will be going somewhere else, my Neshume-le. Closer to God."

I was struck dumb.

"Will I be able to visit you there?" I said, filled with distress.

"No," he told me, "but I will watch over you, and I will bless those who bless you."

—Rachel Naomi Remen, *My Grandfather's Blessings*

For those many of us who have lost loved ones, the greatest comfort is the faith that they are still with us in some unknown way. Today is the day after Valentine's Day 2005. It has been six years since Charlie first got sick and nearly five years since he died. The last few days have been extremely difficult for me, knowing that this day of lovers was approaching, and I have again been struggling with the loneliness, feeling as if I really don't belong anywhere to anyone.

In the midst of all this pain, however, I had a most amazing experience. This morning I was lying in bed, feeling so down and really dreading getting up to begin my day, something very unlike this person (me) whose personal motto is "Spreading Contagious Enthusiasm™!"

As I lay there, I started thinking about a special time several years ago when Charlie and I were laughing and running on the beach here in Florida. He was ahead of me, and all of a sudden, I fell down. Immediately he came back to help me up. At just that moment I actually felt Charlie's arms around me, holding me tightly. Tears began to stream down my face, and I cried, "Oh, Honey, I miss you *so much!*" As he held me close, he whispered in my ear, "Don't lose your joy!" He held me a few moments longer, and then he was gone.

Oh, how precious this experience is to me! It affirms in an other worldly way that he truly *is* still with me, watching over me, just as all your loved ones are a part of your life, too. And best of all, he reminded me of one of the most powerful gifts we can give to our loved ones, both here and in heaven. We need to work through our grief and then we need to find our joy again and keep it in our lives, always focusing on what we have and not on what we don't have. True healing occurs when we can again live our lives in an attitude of joy and perpetual wonder. That is my prayer for each of you who read this book.

As I mentioned at the beginning of this book, it took me a long time to be able to sit down and write it because I realized that I had not fully worked through my own grieving. However, when I did begin, the words simply poured out from my heart and soul and from all those precious people who shared their ideas with me. Not only am I thrilled with how many people I think this book will help, but it has also provided a kind of symbolic closure for me in dealing with my own losses. This work is truly the legacy I leave for my son, husband, father, and all the other loved ones who are no longer with us. May it bless you and help you find peace and healing both as you minister to others and in your own life.

> People are like stained glass windows; they sparkle and shine when the sun is out, but when the darkness sets in, their true beauty is revealed only if there is a light within.
> —Dr. Elisabeth Kübler-Ross

> The most beautiful people we have known are those who have known defeat, known suffering, known struggle, known loss, and have found their way out of the depths. These persons have an appreciation, a sensitivity, and an understanding of life that fills them with compassion, gentleness, and a deep loving concern. Beautiful people do not just happen.
> —Dr. Elisabeth Kübler-Ross

Joyfully,

Barbara

February 2005
Sarasota, Florida

Bibliography

Margaret Metzgar, et al., *A Time to Mourn, A Time to Dance*. Appleton, Wisc.: Aid Association for Lutherans, 2001.

Aldrich, Sandra P. *Will I Ever Be Whole Again? Surviving the Death of Someone You Love*. West Monroe, La.: Howard Publishing Company, 1999.

Balch, Dave. *Cancer for Two*. Twin Peaks, Calif.: A Few Good People, Inc., 2004.

Bendiksen, Robert, ed. *Illness, Crisis, and Loss*. Journal from the Center for Death Education and Bioethics, University of Wisconsin. Lacrosse, Wisc., 2000.

Bernardin, Joseph Cardinal. *The Gift of Peace*. Chicago: Loyola Press, 1997.

Bloomfield, M.D., Harold H. Colgrow, Ph.D., Melba, McWilliams, Peter. *How to Survive the Loss of a Love*. Allen Park, Mich.: Mary Books/Prelude Press, 1976, 1991, 2000.

Bridges, William. *The Way of Transition: Embracing Life's Most Difficult Moments*. Cambridge, Mass.: Perseus Publishing, 2001.

Callanan, Maggie, and Kelley, Patricia. *Final Gifts: Understanding the Special Awareness, Needs, and Communications of the Dying*. New York: Bantam Books, 1997.

Charles, C. Leslie. *All Is Not Lost: The Healing Journey through Crisis, Grief, and Loss*. East Lansing, Mich.: Yes! Press, 2002.

Donnelley, Nina Herrmann. *I Never Know What To Say: How to Help Your Family and Friends Cope with Tragedy*. New York: Ballantine Books, 1987.

Druck, Ken. *Healing Your Life after the Loss of a Loved One*. Spoken word CD. The Heart Talk Series.

Edgar, Robin A. *In My Mother's Kitchen: An Introduction to the Healing Power of Reminisce*. Charlotte, N.C.: Tree House Enterprises, 2003.

Eide, Christine: *Memorial Services Made Easy,* 2003.

Fukmia, Molly. *Safe Passage: Words to Help the Grieving*. Newburyport, Mass.: Red Wheel/Weiser, 2003.

Glen, Genevieve, Kofler, Marilyn, and O'Connor, Kevin. *Handbook for Ministers of Care*. Archdiocese of Chicago: Liturgy Training Publications, 1997.

Greene, Phyllis. *It Must Have Been Moonglow*. New York: Villard Books, 2001.

Grollman, Dr. Earl A. *Living When a Loved One Has Died*. Boston: Beacon Press, 1995.

Hogg, Elaine Ingalls. *Remembering Honey*. www.elainehogg.tripod.com/webpages.

Kelly, Bob. *Heartlifters for the Hurting*. West Monroe, La.: Howard Publishing, 2001.

Klein, Allen. *The Courage to Laugh: Humor, Hope, and Healing in the Face of Death and Dying*. New York: Tarcher/Putnam, 1998.

Lazear, Jonathan. *In the Letting Go: Words to Heal the Heart on the Death of a Father*. Emeryville, Calif.: Conari Press, 2005.

Lazear, Jonathan. *On Love Alone: Words to Heal the Heart on the Death of a Mother*. Emeryville, Calif.: Conari Press, 2005.

Lenskes, Susan. *When Life Takes What Matters: Devotions to Comfort You through Crisis and Change*. Grand Rapids, Mich.: Discovery House Publishers, 1993.

Lester, Andrew D., Ed. *When Children Suffer: A Sourcebook for Ministry with Children*. Philadelphia: The Westminster Press, 1985.

McNamara, Jill Westberg. *My Mom Is Dying: A Child's Diary*. Minneapolis: Augsburg Fortress, 1994.

Noël, N.A. *I Am Wherever You Are*. Indianapolis: Noël Studio, 2000.

Perlitz, Cheryl. *Soaring through Setbacks*. Hilton Head, S.C.: Cameo Publications, 2004.

Prather, Hugh. *The Little Book of Letting Go*. Emeryville, Calif.: Conari Press, 2001.

Rando, Therese A. *How to Go on Living When Someone You Love Dies*. New York: Bantam Books, 1991.

Remen, M.D., Rachel Naomi. *Kitchen Table Wisdom*. New York: Riverhead Books, 1996.

Remen, M.D., Rachel Naomi. *My Grandfather's Blessings*. New York: Riverhead Books, 2000.

Responding to Grief: A Complete Resource Guide. Elgin, Ill.: World Pastoral Care Center, 2001.

Smith, Harold Ivan. *Grievers Ask*. Minneapolis: Augsburg Fortress, 2004.

Smith, James Bryan. *Room of Marvels*. Nashville: B & H Publishers, 2004.

St. Cloud, Terri. *Bone Sighs,* 2002. granolastew@yahoo.com.

Terkel, Studs. *Will the Circle Be Unbroken? Reflections on Death, Rebirth, and Hunger for a Faith*. New York: The New Press, 2001.

Viorst, Judith. *Necessary Losses*. New York: Simon and Schuster, 1986.

Wright, H. Norman. *Experiencing Grief*. Nashville: B&H Publishing Group, 2004.

Wright, H. Norman. *Recovering from the Losses in Life*. Kansas City: Revel, 2006.

York, Sarah. *Remembering Well: Rituals for Celebrating Life and Mourning Death*. San Francisco: Jossey-Bass, 2000.

Ziglar, Zig. *Confessions of a Grieving Christian*. Nashville: Thomas Nelson, 1999.

Zunin, Hilary Stanton, and Leonard M. *The Art of Condolence*. New York: HarperCollins, 1991.

Resources

All of these resources have advice for ways to help the person in pain.

The Cancer Club
6533 Limerick Drive
Edina, MN 55439
www.cancerclub.com

The Compassionate Friends
P. O. Box 3696
Oak Brook, IL 60522-3696
Toll-free: 877-969-0010
Phone: 630-990-0010
Fax: 630-990-0246
www.compassionatefriends.com

Bereaved Parents of the USA
P. O. Box 95
Park Forest, IL 60466
Phone: 708-748-7866
www.bereavedparentsusa.org

World Pastoral Care Center
Father Richard Gilbert
1030 Summit Street, Suite 338
Elgin, IL 60120
E-mail: dick.gilbert@shermanhospital.org.

Grief Digest Magazine
P. O. Box 4600
Omaha, NE 68104
Phone: 402-553-1200
Fax: 402-553-0507
E-mail: centeringcorp@aol.com
www.centering.org

Centre for Education about Death and Bereavement
King's college, London, Ontario
www.wwdc.com/death

Bereavement, A Magazine of Hope and Healing
8133 Telegraph Drive
Colorado Springs, CO 80920-7169
Phone: 719-282-1948
Fax: 719-282-1850
E-mail: grief@usa.net

Center for Death Education and Bioethics
Soc/Arc Department
435 NH
University of Wisconsin
Lacrosse, WI 54601-3742
Phone: 608-785-6781
E-mail: CDEB@uwlax.edu

Walking the Mourner's Path, a Christ-centered approach to "secondary grief"—grief that happens weeks, months, years after the initial death.
www.mournerspath.com

www.petloss.com, when a pet is ill or dies

www.griefnet.org, an Internet community of persons dealing with grief, death, and major loss.

www.musicalreflections.com, Tami Briggs, Therapeutic Harpist.
Phone: 952-829-1919
Fax: 952-829-0985
"Touching a Chord to Orchestrate Healing"

Acknowledgments

The author would like to thank the following for giving us permission to print their stories in this book:

Darla Arni, Mirna Audet, Joanne Ax, Kim Barnhill, Bruce Bauerle, Jean Becker, Christine Clifford Beckwith, Dan Bent, Linnea Berg, Pam Blankenship, John Blumberg, Lonnie Lee Bone, Karna Burkeen, Jack and Pam Burks, Tom Burley, Mark Camacho, Darrah Casperson, Leslie Charles, Nancy Cobb, Carol Jo DeFore, Kathy (Morrison) Ditlevson, Sandy Donaldson, Patricia Duffy, Lynn Durham, Elissa Ecker, Alyice Edrich, Rita Emmett, Belle Fangmeyer, Jim Feldman, Jeff Fendley, Davis Fisher, Jim Flynn, Valla Dana Fotiades, Ruth Gagnon, Arthur Gershowitz, Garrett and Ashley Glanz, Carol Goldsmith, Annie Gourley, T. Scott Gross, Deb Haggerty, Curt Hansen, Peter Hart, Kathie Hightower, Elaine Ingalls Hogg, Steve Holtzer, Patti Homan, Patsy Jacoy, Rick Jakle, Janie Jasin, Shannon Johnston, Jane Jones, Sporty King, Edith Kmet, Tina Kreminski, Jan Krouskop, Margie Kruk, Jane Kucera, Lori Kwasniewski, Ben La Corte, Phyllis Landstrom, Carol Kramer Leiphart, Joe Liss, Al Lucia, Scott Marcus, Cyndy Maxey, Robin Maynard, the Michelini family, Mary Nelson, Sheryl Nicholson, Colleen Nordlund, Shirley Ottman, Kathy Pacey, Roy Parnell, Cheryl Pence, Cheryl Perlitz, Barry Pitegoff, Ginger Plowman, Michael Poll, Debbie Preuss, Lynette Reick, Rosemarie Rosetti, David Roth, Karen Rowinsky, Lanette Salisbury, Irene and Roy Saunderson, the David Schulz family, Kathy Schuster, Patt Schwab, Amy Segami, Beverly Smallwood, Kate Sorenson, Justin Spring, Storeebrooke, Cheryl Stubbendieck, Ana Tampanna, Carol Copeland Thomas, Oralee Thompson, Jeff Tobe, Angelo and Linda Tomasello, Dr. Anju Tripathi Peters, Bud Verdi, Michelle Voller, Penny Wallace, Sandy Wasik, Denise White, June Wilson, Karen Yoho

Introduction and Notes to Readers

Page 15: Barbara Lazear Ascher, *Landscape Without Gravity: A Memoir of Grief* (Delphinium Books, 1992).

Page 15: Oswald Chambers, *My Utmost for His Highest* (Grand Rapids, Mich.: Discovery House, 1992), 45.

Page 16: Andrea Gambill, editor of *Grief Digest* and founder of *Bereavement* magazine.

Page 16: George Eliot, excerpt from "Middlemarch." George Eliot is the pen name of Mary Anne Evans, English novelist (1819–1880).

Page 21: Charles Dickens, *Great Expectations* (1860–1861).

Page 22: *When Life Takes What Matters,* © 1993 by Susan Lenzkes. Used by permission of Discovery House Publishers, Box 3566, Grand Rapids, MI 49501. All rights reserved. Used by permission.

Page 23: Anne Lamott, *Plan B: Further Thoughts on Faith* (New York: Riverhead Books, 2005).

Chapter 1

Page 24: Henri Nouwen, *Out of Solitude* (Notre Dame, Ind.: Ave Maria, 1974), 34.

Page 24: Charles R. Swindoll, *Killing Giants, Pulling Thorns* (Grand Rapids, Mich.: Zondervan, 1994).

Page 30: Henry Scott Holland (1847–1918), Canon of Christ Church, Oxford.

Page 35: Terri St. Cloud, "She Understood" from *Bone Sighs* (Accokeek, Md.: Bone Sigh Arts, 2002).

Chapter 2

Page 36: John Eldredge, *Wild at Heart: Discovering the Secret of a Man's Soul* (Nashville: Thomas Nelson, 2003).

Chapter 3

Page 38: *Living When a Loved One Has Died* by Earl A. Grollman. Copyright © 1977 by Earl A. Grollman. Reprinted by permission of Beacon Press, Boston.

Page 46: Christine Clifford Beckwith, *Cancer Has its Privileges: Stories of Hope and Laughter* (New York: Perigee, 2002).

Chapter 5
Page 54: *Talking about Death* by Earl A. Grollman. Copyright © 1990 by Earl A. Grollman. Reprinted by permission of Beacon Press, Boston.

Chapter 6
Page 64: Tom Ehrich, "On a Journey," Journey Publishing Company, www.onajourney.org.

Page 64: C. S. Lewis, *A Grief Observed* (New York: Harper, 1961).

Page 64: *Meditations of the Heart* by Howard Thurman. Copyright © 1953, 1981 by Anne Thurman. Reprinted by permission of Beacon Press, Boston.

Chapter 7
Page 72: Dana Reeve, in "Do Something for Someone" by Lisa Birnbach, *Parade,* May 1, 2005 (New York: Parade Publications, 2005).

Page 72: Brendan Francis Behan (Irish playwright, 1923–1964).

Page 72: Billy Graham, *Hope for the Troubled Heart* (New York: Bantam, 1993), 100.

Page 79: "Break, Break, Break," Lord Alfred Tennyson (1809–1892).

Chapter 8
Page 82: Susan Squellati Florence, *When You Lose Someone You Love: A Journey through the Heart of Grief* (Watford, Herts, UK: Exley Publications Ltd., 2002).

Page 82: Edith Kmet, "To a Compassionate Friend." Reprinted by permission of the author.

Page 83: Mary S. Cleckley, *I Walked a Mile in Sorrow* (Omaha: The Centering Corp., 2006). Reprinted by permission of the author.

Page 90: Sandra L. Graves, *What to Do When a Loved One Dies* (Irving, Calif.: Dickens Press, 1994).

Chapter 9

Page 91: Nona Martin Stuck, "The Face of Grief" in *O, The Oprah Magazine*, August 1, 2003, (New York: Hearst Communications, 2003).

Page 98: *Living When a Loved One Has Died* by Earl A. Grollman. Copyright © 1977 by Earl A. Grollman. Reprinted by permission of Beacon Press, Boston.

Chapter 10

Page 99: "And If I Go," Emily Dickinson (1830–1886).

Chapter 11

Page 107: Mitch Albom, *Tuesdays with Morrie* (New York: Doubleday, 1997), 174.

Page 107: Frederick Buechner, *Whistling in the Dark* (New York: Harper & Row, 1988), 100.

Page 107: Linda Zelenka, "Older Grief." © Linda Zelenka. Reprinted by permission.

Page 113: Reprinted with permission from *Bereavement* magazine, 8133 Telegraph Drive, Colorado Springs, CO 80920 and Barbara A. Glanz, *Care Packages for the Home—Dozens of Ways to Regenerate Spirit Where You Live* (Kansas City, Mo.: Andrews McMeel, 1998.)

Chapter 12

Page 124: Og Mandino, *A Better Way to Live* (New York: Bantam, 1990), 90.

Chapter 13

Page 132: Margaret H. Gerner, poem from *For Bereaved Grandparents* (Omaha: The Centering Corp., 1990). Used by permission.

Chapter 14

Page 140: Thomas Campbell, Scottish poet (1777–1844), from "Hallowed Ground."

Page 140: Alfred Montapert, American author (1906–).

Chapter 15

Page 146: Sascha Wagner, *Wintersun*. Reprinted by permission of The Compassionate Friends, Oakbrook, Ill.

Page 146: Robert N. Test, "To Remember Me" reprinted courtesy of The Living Bank, PO Box 6725, Houston, TX 77265

Chapter 16

Page 155: Poem © Terri Kelly. Used by permission.

Conclusion

Page 162: Rachel Naomi Remen, from *My Grandfather's Blessings: Stories of Strength, Refuge and Belonging* (New York: Riverhead Books, 2000).

Page 163: Dr. Elisabeth Kübler-Ross. Reprinted by permission. www.elisabethkublerross.com and www.ekrfoundation.

Page 163: Dr. Elisabeth Kübler-Ross. Reprinted by permission. www.elisabethkublerross.com and www.ekrfoundation.